D0687999

The Columbine School Shootings

Other titles in the Crime Scene Investigations series:

WITHDRAWN

The Columbine School Shootings

by Jenny MacKay

LUCENT BOOKS

A part of Gale, Cengage Learning

GALE
CENGAGE Learning™

Detroit • New York • San Francisco • New Haven, Conn • Waterville, Maine • London

LIBRARY OF CONGRESS CATALOGING-IN-PUBLICATION DATA

Mackay, Jenny.
   The Columbine School shooting / by Jenny MacKay.
     p. cm. -- (Crime scene investigations)
   Includes bibliographical references and index.
   ISBN 978-1-4205-0138-4 (hardcover)
   1. Columbine High School Massacre, Littleton, Colo., 1999--Juvenile
literature. 2. School shootings--Colorado--Littleton--Juvenile literature.
3. Columbine High School (Littleton, Colo.)--Juvenile literature.
   I. Title.
    LB3013.33.C6M33 2010
    373.17'820978882—dc22

                                   2009036532

Lucent Books
27500 Drake Rd
Farmington Hills MI 48331

ISBN-13: 978-1-4205-0138-4
ISBN-10: 1-4205-0138-0

Printed in the United States of America
2 3 4 5 6 7 13 12 11 10

Printed by Bang Printing, Brainerd, MN, 2nd Ptg., 12/2010

Contents

Foreword

The popularity of crime scene and investigative crime shows on television has come as a surprise to many who work in the field. The main surprise is the concept that crime-scene analysts are the true crime solvers, when in truth, it takes dozens of people, doing many different jobs, to solve a crime. Often, the crime-scene analyst's contribution is a small one. One Minnesota forensic scientist says that the public "has gotten the wrong idea. Because I work in a lab similar to the ones on *CSI*, people seem to think I'm solving crimes left and right—just me and my microscope. They don't believe me when I tell them that it's just the investigators that are solving crimes, not me."

Crime-scene analysts do have an important role to play, however. Science has rapidly added a whole new dimension to gathering and assessing evidence. Modern crime labs can match a hair of a murder suspect to one found on a murder victim, for example, or recover a fingerprint from a threatening letter, or use a powerful microscope to match tool marks made during the wiring of an explosive device to a tool in a suspect's possession.

Probably the most exciting of the forensic scientist's tools is DNA analysis. DNA can be found in just one drop of blood, in a dribble of saliva on a toothbrush, or even in the residue from a fingerprint. Some DNA analysis techniques enable scientists to tell with certainty, for example, whether a drop of blood on a suspect's shirt is from a murder victim.

While these exciting techniques are now an essential part of many investigations, they cannot solve crimes alone. "DNA doesn't come with a name and address on it," says the Minnesota forensic scientist. "It's great if you have someone in custody to match the sample to, but otherwise, it doesn't help.

That's the investigator's job. We can have all the great DNA evidence in the world, and without a suspect, it will just sit on a shelf. We've all seen cases with very little forensic evidence get solved by the resourcefulness of a detective."

While forensic specialists get the most media attention today, the work of detectives still forms the core of most criminal investigations. Their job, in many ways, has changed little over the years. Most cases are still solved through the persistence and determination of a detective whose work may be anything but glamorous. Many cases require routine, even mind-numbing tasks. After the July 2005 bombings in London, for example, police officers sat in front of monitors watching thousands of hours of closed-circuit television tape from security cameras throughout the city, and as a result were able to get images of the bombers.

The Lucent Books Crime Scene Investigations series explores the variety of ways crimes are solved. Titles cover particular crimes, such as murder; specific cases, such as the killing of three civil rights workers in Mississippi; or the role specialists, such as medical examiners play in solving crimes. Each title in the series demonstrates the ways a crime may be solved, from the various applications of forensic science and technology to the reasoning of investigators. Sidebars examine both the limits and possibilities of the new technologies and present crime statistics, career information, and step-by-step explanations of scientific and legal processes.

The Crime Scene Investigations series strives to be both informative and realistic about how members of law enforcement—criminal investigators, forensic scientists, and others—solve crimes, for it is essential that student researchers understand that crime solving is rarely quick or easy. Many factors—from a detective's dogged pursuit of one tenuous lead to a suspect's careless mistake to sheer luck to complex calculations computed in the lab—are all part of crime solving today.

A School Under Attack

On April 20, 1999, two seniors at Columbine High School in Jefferson County, Colorado, went to school with guns, knives, and bombs concealed beneath their trench coats and opened fire on their classmates and teachers. In less than an hour, they detonated thirty handmade bombs, shot and killed twelve students and a teacher, and injured twenty-three others.

At the time, the massacre at Columbine High School was the deadliest school shooting that had ever taken place in America. News vans and helicopters descended on the scene moments after the attack began, and people all over the country watched events unfold live on television. Groups of teachers and students escaped from the school throughout the afternoon, and police officers herded them to safety far away from the campus. None of the police officers went into the school for the better part of an hour, and by the time they did, the two killers had already shot and killed themselves in the school library.

The way police responded to Columbine and later processed the crime scene and investigated the shootings became a study of what to do and what not to do during a shooting rampage at a school—an event that has occurred in American schools with increasing frequency since the early 1990s. Police officers from more than thirty different departments and law enforcement agencies responded to Columbine High School just minutes after the first shots were fired, and they did exactly what they had been trained to do—surround the building, help people to safety, get information from witnesses, and wait for the Special Weapons and Tactics (SWAT) teams to arrive and enter the building in search of the shooters.

However, many difficulties arose during the police response to Columbine. The SWAT teams that entered the school had

rushed to the scene so quickly that they lacked important equipment, such as bulletproof vests and gun shields. The sheriff's office was unprepared to handle an event of such magnitude, and there were no maps available of the school that could have aided the SWAT teams' search. Radio airways were so overwhelmed with calls by other law enforcement officers that the SWAT teams could not communicate with each other by radio. The school's fire alarms blared, which made it impossible for SWAT officers to hear anything within the school, and no one had known how to turn them off. Under these circumstances, it took SWAT teams hours to search the classrooms and hallways of the school's lower level before they could get upstairs and find the two dead gunmen and their victims.

Some were critical of how the SWAT teams handled the Columbine High School shootings.

Although they followed their training procedures precisely in an unpredictable situation with unforeseen challenges, these officers were later criticized harshly because they did not enter the school immediately and stop the killers. Critics of the police response said some of the victims might have been saved if police had been better prepared for such a situation. Since the shootings at Columbine, many of the country's police departments are now trained in how to respond to a school shooting and they are prepared to enter a school immediately to stop a shooter.

The police responders were not the only ones criticized. Investigators who studied the crime uncovered surprising things about the killers, including the fact that both gunmen had been arrested for breaking into a vehicle a year before their attack. One of the gunmen had also been reported to police for a violent Web site he created that detailed his murderous intentions. But the Jefferson County Sheriff's Office never followed up with a search warrant for the teenager's computer, an action that might have alerted police to what he was up to.

Many wondered how two teenagers were able to obtain so much weaponry, including these guns and rounds of ammunition.

There was also controversy surrounding how the two teenagers were able to get the four guns they used to kill and injure dozens of their fellow students. Some people criticized the violent video games, movies, and music that the killers had loved. These people blamed the media for inflaming murderous rage

in America's teens. Lawsuits filed after the attack sought justice for the victims, but most of these lawsuits were eventually thrown out by a Jefferson County judge who decided that the gunmen's actions could not fairly be blamed on anyone else.

Critics also focused on the killers' teachers and peers, asking if anyone had noticed anything suspicious about the two teens. Since the attack at Columbine, teachers and administrators around the country have attended training programs to learn how to detect warning signs that a student might attempt a school shooting. Today's teachers and students are much more wary of violent statements and threatening behavior as a result of the Columbine shootings.

In the decade after the shootings at Columbine, much changed in America, both in law enforcement and in schools. The incident at Columbine High School stood as the deadliest school shooting in American history until 2007, when a student at Virginia Tech tragically took thirty-three lives before ending his own. Today the massacre at Columbine serves as a reminder for communities, law enforcement, and schools to remain vigilant and to be prepared in case the unthinkable happens again.

CHAPTER 1

The Emergency Response

April 20, 1999, was a sunny spring day in Jefferson County, Colorado, 10 miles (16km) outside the city of Denver. As usual, officers of the Jefferson County Sheriff's Office were patrolling the community, a suburb consisting of friendly neighborhoods, quiet streets, a few strip malls, and very little crime. They had no idea that they would soon be responding to reports of gunfire in one of the area's schools. It would turn out to be a situation that they had never faced before and one for which they were unprepared.

A Single Explosion

It was a quiet day at Columbine High School, home to nearly two thousand students, the Rebels mascot, and several championship sports teams. About the time students were being let out of class for the first lunch period, a call came in to the county's 911 dispatch office from a community citizen who had just seen a bomb explode in a grassy field off Wadsworth Boulevard, about 3 miles (4.8km) southwest of the school. At 11:21 A.M., Deputy Paul Magor was dispatched to the scene of that explosion to investigate. No one at Columbine High School was aware of the bomb.

Lunchroom Commotion

About the time Deputy Magor was responding to the explosion in the field, a custodian at Columbine noticed something going on outside the lunchroom. Students who had the first lunch period were congregating at the windows to get a look at whatever was happening outside. The custodian picked up his campus radio and made a call to Deputy Neil Gardner, the

Columbine High School's 2,000 students were not prepared for what was about to happen to them on April 20, 1999.

COLUMBINE HIGH SCHOOL

COLUMBINE HIGH SCHOOL

HOME OF THE
REBELS

The Dead

The following thirteen people were shot and killed at Columbine High School on April 20, 1999.

Cassie Bernall, age 18
Steven Curnow, age 14
Corey DePooter, age 17
Kelly Fleming, age 16
Matthew Kechter, age 16
Daniel Mauser, age 15
Dan Rohrbough, age 15
Rachel Scott, age 17
Isaiah Shoels, age 18
John Tomlin, age 16
Lauren Townsend, age 18
Kyle Velasquez, age 16
Dave Sanders, teacher, age 47

community resource officer who worked at Columbine. The custodian told Gardner to hurry to the back lot of the school. Fearing that a student may have been hit by a vehicle, Gardner put his patrol car in gear and circled the campus, heading for the south parking lot.

At the same time, a call came over the police radio dispatch system about a female being down in the south parking lot of the school. Deputy Gardner activated the lights and siren on his patrol car as he drove toward the scene. A few miles away on Wadsworth Boulevard, Deputy Magor heard the same call over his radio.

Police officers are trained to react to many different situations. All of them require a calm approach so the officer can properly assess a situation before taking action. "The health, safety and psychological well-being of personnel who staff a major disaster is an important consideration for those charged with coordination of the investigation and recovery efforts,"[1] says Barry A. J. Fisher, the crime laboratory director for the Los Angeles County Sheriff's Department. A dead or injured police officer is no help to anyone.

Shots Fired

After arriving in the south parking lot at 11:24 A.M., Deputy Gardner stepped out of his patrol car and saw two teenagers holding guns outside the west doors of the school building. Gardner immediately drew his own firearm. One of the gunmen turned toward him and aimed his rifle, shooting at Gardner ten times before the rifle jammed. All shots missed Gardner and he returned fire, shooting four times without hitting his target.

Police arriving at Columbine had very little information about what was happening inside the school.

The gunman and his partner then disappeared inside the school. Gardner called for backup on his radio at 11:26 A.M. Just five minutes had passed since the 911 call reported the explosion in a field 3 miles (4.8km) away.

In response to Gardner's call, other officers in the vicinity sped to the school. As two deputies arrived in the west parking lot, one of the gunmen leaned out a broken window and shot at the officers with a rifle. The deputies returned fire, and the gunman retreated inside. By this time, panicked students were beginning to flee the building. The two deputies in the west parking lot could hear more gunfire coming from inside the school, but they had no idea who the shooters were, how many of them were in the building, or what they intended to do. The officers followed procedure and surrounded the school and waited for more backup.

"When the Columbine incident occurred in Colorado, first responder officers did what was traditionally recommended, which was to form a perimeter and wait for the arrival of the SWAT [Special Weapons and Tactics] team," says David B. Stein a psychology professor at Longwood University in Virginia and a consultant to the Virginia State Police. Under those recommendations, "a squadron of patrol cars converges at the school as quickly as possible," Stein says, in order to form a "protective perimeter around the students."[2]

At 11:27 A.M., from the south parking lot, Deputy Gardner again radioed for assistance. In the west parking lot, two officers set up roadblocks to seal off the exits from the school. At 11:29 A.M., the sheriff's office dispatch alerted all available police units that there were officers under fire at Columbine High School. For the next seven minutes, the deputies on the west side of the building could hear gunfire coming from the library on the second floor of the school. During this time, gunmen inside the building also shot at officers from the west-facing library windows, and the officers returned fire. Meanwhile, students fleeing the school were taking cover behind police cars that had arrived at the scene. Some officers began driving carloads of students away from campus so that they would not be injured by the gunfire.

The Shift to Emergency Mode

By 11:30 A.M., so many 911 calls were flooding the sheriff's office dispatchers that the dispatch center switched to emergency command mode, enlisting the help of additional people to deal with the panicked calls coming in from the school. In the first forty minutes of the attack, according to the official Jefferson County Sheriff's report, "dispatch received 31 emergency calls from people inside and outside the school relating information about the Columbine incident…. Dispatchers had no time to verify the reports coming at them. They disseminated all the information received back to the command post and to the deputies on scene."[3] Meanwhile, the Littleton Fire Department was sent to the scene to begin treating the injured. At 11:31 A.M., an officer radioed in that there was smoke coming from the building. A moment later, the first fire alarm went off inside the school.

Several police officers as well as SWAT responded to the scene after the gunmen opened fire on police.

By 11:35 A.M., just twelve minutes after the school custodian had radioed Gardner for help, deputies from neighboring police departments in Denver and the City of Littleton were arriving at the scene, and the Jefferson County SWAT commander was on his way, along with several SWAT teams from surrounding police departments. By 11:36 A.M., a SWAT team command post was established near the school. "Chaos played a big part," say journalists who later recapped the events of that day in an article for *TIME* magazine. "From the moment of the first report of gunshots at Columbine, SWAT team members raced in from every direction, some without their equipment, some in jeans and t-shirts, just trying to get there quickly."[4]

By now, multiple explosions could be heard coming from the school, one of them blowing out cafeteria windows. Concerned that the suspects might try to escape by blending in with the crowds of students fleeing the school, several police officers kept the campus surrounded. Other officers helped evacuate students, some of whom had been injured. Still other officers were directing traffic away from the school. The media had arrived, and curious onlookers and frantic parents were beginning to surround the high school.

A Complicated Crime Scene

When police officers respond to a situation like the Columbine High School massacre, their first priority is to prevent fatalities. An organized and well-planned response to a violent situation involving guns and explosives is crucial to keeping injuries and deaths to a minimum. At the scene of major incidents, all responding law enforcement are under the direction of an on-site commander, who has the responsibility of assessing the overall

Becoming an Emergency Dispatcher

Job Description
Emergency dispatchers work in a dispatch call center to answer 911 calls from the public and to dispatch police, fire, and ambulance services as necessary. They also coordinate radio traffic between emergency workers on several radio channels, maintain contact with all police and emergency units that are on call, and keep track of the location of police and fire units at all times.

Education
Graduation from high school is the minimum educational requirement, although classes taken at a vocational school will increase the chances of finding employment.

Qualifications
Emergency dispatchers need to be computer literate and able to operate a variety of programs, phone systems, and radio equipment efficiently. They must have excellent map skills and be able to accurately type at least 35 words per minute while transcribing spoken dialogue. Candidates must also have excellent hearing and vision. They must demonstrate an ability to work well in stressful situations and to prioritize tasks according to the level of emergency.

Additional Information
Emergency dispatchers must be willing to work a variety of shifts, including evenings, weekends, and holidays, and are often on call even during their days off. Job applicants are required to complete a variety of performance tests to gauge their ability to do this kind of work.

Salary
$25,000 to $40,000 per year

SWAT preparing to enter the school did not know how many gunmen were in the building or where they were located.

situation and giving orders to specific officers to carry out certain duties. "The incident commander at such a scene has one goal: to save lives," says Dennis R. Krebs of the Baltimore County Fire Department in Maryland. "A unified command ... will need to assemble at a joint command post to manage the incident."[5]

This is precisely what took place at Columbine. Police officers from multiple police departments descended on the school, and within half an hour of when the first shots were fired, a central command post had been established and officers were standing by, ready to take orders. But commanding officers were still unsure of what exactly was going on inside the building. Dozens of 911 calls from students and teachers, some who had escaped and some who were still trapped inside the school, gave conflicting reports of what was happening. Some callers said there were two shooters. Some said there were as many as eight. Reports of bombs and fires and semiautomatic weapons flooded dispatchers. Calls came in so quickly that it was impossible to pin down exactly how many assailants were involved, where they were in the school, what weapons they carried, and whether they could be trying to escape.

The lack of reliable information about the number of shooters made it difficult for police SWAT teams to prepare to enter the school. "Knowing the number of shooters is extremely important for officers," says Stein. "If they neutralize one, and there are really two, the police can be caught off guard and placed at great peril."[6] The SWAT officers were also hindered by not knowing where they might find the suspects once they entered the school. And although SWAT teams typically train with members of their own team, they do not train with members of other teams. In their haste to reach the scene, teams were incomplete and new teams had to be formed on the spot. Some of the SWAT officers were strangers to each other. Many also did not have their bulletproof vests and other protective equipment with them, because SWAT officers in small communities like Jefferson County usually work on call and do not carry their SWAT gear everywhere. Instead, they report to police headquarters if an emergency arises, collect their SWAT gear, and get briefed on the situation. Not only were many SWAT officers who responded to Columbine off duty and unequipped at the time of the call, they were dispatched directly to Columbine High School in the confusion, rather than to police headquarters to collect their gear.

As SWAT officers hastily gathered outside Columbine, the sounds of gunfire and explosions continued to come from the school. The shooters had exchanged fire with officers on one side of the building, then the other. Smoke poured from windows that had broken during one explosion. Some officers, as they helped fleeing students, began asking questions that might give them a better idea of what was going on inside. "Although these people may be distraught, they can also be excellent sources of information," says Krebs. "Can they describe the suspect(s), including height, weight, and clothing? Where is the suspect located in the building? What type and number of weapons are being used? How many people are injured?"[7] The responding officers obtained as much information as they could from escapees. But within thirty minutes of the start of the ordeal, there were officers from so many departments at the scene and so much traffic on the radios that sharing the information back and forth became as chaotic as the situation itself.

"Where are the shootings occurring and in what direction are the shooters heading?" Stein asks. "Answers to these help responding officers head directly toward the threat without wasting valuable time."[8] But the SWAT officers responding to Columbine did not have this vital information.

SWAT Teams Advance

Despite the state of confusion surrounding the school, the Jefferson County Sheriff's Office authorized SWAT teams to enter the building at 11:52 A.M., half an hour into the attack. By that time, the building's fire sprinkler system and fire alarms had been activated. Strobe lights flashed. The shrill sound of the fire alarms was unnerving and made it impossible for the SWAT teams to communicate verbally with each other or to hear whether anyone might be approaching them. The teams were unsure how many suspects they were searching for, how heavily the shooters were armed, or where they were in the building. "The local lawmen didn't know what they were dealing with,"[9] said Bill Owens, the governor of Colorado at the time of the shootings at Columbine.

Another problem SWAT faced: None of the officers was familiar with the layout of the two-story, 250,000-square-foot school. Not knowing where they were going or who exactly they were looking for, the first SWAT teams made their way into the smoky halls, one team going in through the southeast entrance, the other entering from the west side of the school.

Evacuating Columbine

The two SWAT teams entering at opposite ends of the school knew very few things for certain. They had been warned of live bombs, multiple shooters, and a possible hostage situation (which turned out to be untrue—at no point were the killers interested in holding hostages). Gunfire and explosions had

The Boy in the Window

Of all the images captured on film on that horrible day at Columbine High School, the footage of a teenager climbing out of a library window is among the most vivid. The student was seventeen-year-old Patrick Ireland, a junior who had gone to the library at lunch that day to study. While hiding from the gunmen, Ireland was shot in the right foot. Then, when he was giving first aid to another student, he was shot in the head.

Hours after the start of the attacks, rescuers outside noticed Ireland trying to get out of a broken window. SWAT officers drove an armored vehicle alongside the school, and two officers stood on the roof of the vehicle to catch Ireland as he tumbled headfirst out the window.

His head injury caused brain damage which partially paralyzed Ireland. He had to relearn to walk, talk, read, and write. A year later, he graduated as valedictorian of his senior class. Ireland attended Colorado State University, graduated with honors, married his college sweetheart, and now works as a financial planner, rarely thinking of the day he almost died at Columbine.

Patrick Ireland jumping out of the library window.

been reported from nearly every wing of the school building. The school was littered with bodies, some dead, others critically wounded. The halls were filled with noise and smoke. Live pipe bombs were strewn everywhere. Some areas were flooded with several inches of water where the fire sprinklers had gone off.

As SWAT moved through Columbine, students were evacuated out of the school.

Broken ceiling tiles made eerie holes overhead, leaving SWAT teams wary of shooters who might be hiding up above. Wires dangled from the ceiling. The walls in the school's main entrance were riddled with bullet holes. A strange hissing noise aroused one SWAT team's concern that a natural gas line may have broken and could be leaking gas inside the school.

Students and teachers still inside the building had locked and barricaded themselves into classrooms. As SWAT teams moved through the school, every door had to be opened and every room searched for survivors, hostages, or killers. As survivors were found, they were escorted out of established rescue exits, pathways that had been cleared of bombs and other dangers. Police officers waited outside the rescue exits to receive and help the people being evacuated.

In the kitchen area alone, there were twenty to thirty students hiding, along with two adults who had shut themselves into the walk-in freezer and were so cold they could hardly move their arms. Students being evacuated out of one rescue exit had to pass the bodies of two dead students, and police officers had the responsibility of keeping the evacuees from looking at the bodies and suffering even more emotional trauma.

Almost sixty students were hiding in a closet in the music room. Across the hall, another sixty hid in classrooms. Fifty to sixty more were hiding in the science wing. The students were so terrified that they would not open the doors when the SWAT teams knocked, fearing that the officers were the killers returning to shoot at them. The fire alarm noise made it difficult for SWAT teams to communicate with the students, many of whom were afraid to follow the officers out of the school. SWAT officers were still on the lookout for shooters and wary of booby traps and live bombs. It took hours for SWAT teams to search every classroom, storage closet, and hallway to make sure more attackers were not lying in wait to ambush the emergency rescue teams that were desperately needed by the dying.

Outside, Still Waiting

While SWAT teams searched the school's interior, the area outside the building looked like a war zone. Television news crews were everywhere. News helicopters hovered in the skies, broadcasting live aerial shots of the school to a nation now riveted to television sets as it watched the massacre in Colorado unfold. Dozens of ambulances, fire trucks, and other emergency vehicles surrounded the school and filled neighboring Clement Park, where the wounded were being transported. Some awaited helicopter transport to area hospitals. SWAT officers had climbed to the rooftops of houses on the streets surrounding Columbine to get a better view of what was happening at the school. Armored vehicles carrying police officers were pulling up close to the school to pick up groups of evacuated students and take them out of harm's way. A student named Patrick Ireland, critically injured and desperate to escape from the second-floor library, began climbing out a window. Quick-thinking rescuers steered an armored vehicle to the side of the school and stood on its roof to catch the teenager as he fell.

For several hours, the fearful scene was broadcast live on news stations throughout the country. Columbine High School is in an upper-middle-class, heavily religious Colorado suburb with a very low rate of crime. It is a school filled with honor students, church groups, and state champion sports teams. If a school shooting could happen at Columbine, journalists said, it could happen anywhere.

At 4:45 P.M., five and a half hours after the first emergency calls were made to the Jefferson County Sheriff's Office, SWAT teams had cleared the building of all known victims still hiding out in classrooms and other spaces. In all, twelve students, one teacher, and the two gunmen lay dead inside the school. In addition to the dead and injured, there were numerous pipe bombs and other explosives throughout the school as well as in the two killers' cars in the parking lot. Police worried that additional killers could still be in the school, hiding out in crawl spaces or storage areas in order to attack medical and forensic personnel coming into the crime scene. To ensure that the school was safe, SWAT teams made a second sweep of the building and grounds before various emergency medical and law enforcement personnel began entering the school—those who would tend to the injured, those who would process the crime scene, and those who would identify the fifteen people who were dead.

Processing the Scene

By late afternoon, emergency medical personnel were helping critically injured victims still inside the school, and crime scene investigators were collecting evidence for the questions that would need answers in the days and weeks to come: who committed the crime, how did they do it, and perhaps most pressing, why did they do it. The job was immense, and the work was painstaking. Investigators did not want to miss anything important. Yet, the public pressed for speed and questioned the length of time it seemed to take investigators to get anything done.

Victims in Need

To the media crews hovering outside and to millions of people watching coverage of the horrific event on television, it seemed like long hours passed with no one doing anything. A disturbing, handwritten sign in a window read, "1 bleeding to death." It did not seem as if any rescuers were flooding in to save this person or the countless others who might be inside, clinging to the last moments of life. It was something that critics of the investigation later claimed was inexcusable. "The families of the dead and injured shooting victims ... argued that the sheriff's deputies should have and could have done more to protect the victims,"[10] according to one report that aired on a local news station.

What no one on the outside could see was the sheer amount of damage that had been done inside the enormous, two-story high school. The place reeked of smoke and was peppered with spent bullet casings and shattered glass from broken windows. Portions of ceilings and walls were demolished. Dozens of abandoned backpacks floated among the lunch tables in the

Rescue workers were forced to wait outside the school instead of entering to treat the wounded due to possible bombs.

cafeteria, one of the areas that had been flooded with several inches of water when the fire sprinklers were activated. The SWAT teams had been warned about bombs in some of the backpacks, but they had no idea which ones. There was bloodstained carpet in the hallways, and blood was smeared on some of the walls. As SWAT teams cleared the building, no one knew for certain how many gunmen had been inside the school or whether dangerous individuals were still lying in wait in hallways or classrooms.

During the SWAT sweeps, rescue workers waited outside in the staging area, a control center that had been established at a safe distance from the school. To the news cameras, it looked as if they were ignoring the sign in the window, but they were following orders from deputies. Dennis R. Krebs of the Baltimore County Fire Department in Maryland explains, "If rescuers enter an area where a gunman is still loose, the rescuers can be injured by gunfire." He also says, "Another reason for keeping fire and rescue personnel in the staging area is the possibility that the suspect(s) may have planted explosives and other booby traps."[11] Law enforcement was following standard procedure by not allowing emergency medical personnel into what was still a very dangerous and unpredictable crime scene. To send them into a hazardous area without first eliminating dangers would have been irresponsible and could have led to even more loss of life. And, as it turned out, while the gunmen were found dead, nearly one hundred explosive devices were also eventually found inside the school. So for hours, while SWAT teams searched, medical professionals waited tensely outside for the go-ahead to enter the building and help the injured.

Finding Bodies

After hours of searching by SWAT teams, investigators finally determined that the only two people in the school who were armed and dangerous were already dead. The killers had

Disaster Support at Columbine

During the afternoon of the shootings, thousands of people converged on Columbine High School. Emergency responders, the media, and the families of missing students were among those who remained close to the scene for hours, many of them staying overnight. Both the Red Cross and the Salvation Army were on-site, providing food and water, blankets, clothing, portable toilets, and heaters for those who remained at the school. Warm meals and dry clothes were invaluable comforts for those who remained at the scene, especially when a late-spring snowstorm hit the area during the week after the attack. The Colorado Restaurant Association and local grocery stores donated food. For ten days, volunteers from the Red Cross and the Salvation Army remained at Columbine, serving a total of 27,000 meals to victims, families, investigators, and responders.

By the Numbers

2,942

Number of hours investigators spent interviewing witnesses in the two weeks after the shooting at Columbine

chosen the library as the scene for their suicide, the same place where they killed and injured the majority of their victims. Ten murdered teenagers lay in the room, students who had huddled together beneath tables, helpless against the killers' bullets.

When the main areas of the school had been cleared of danger from explosives, medical professionals were finally allowed to enter the scene and assist with the "one bleeding to death," a science teacher named Dave Sanders who had been shot in the neck and chest while urging students to run for cover. A group of students had barricaded themselves into a classroom with Sanders, and for hours, they did all they could to staunch the bleeding from his wounds. They also placed the sign in the classroom window to tell officers of Sanders' dire condition.

According to the official sheriff's report, SWAT teams had known that the person bleeding to death must be somewhere on the upper level, "since SWAT had just finished clearing the lower floor" and had not yet found him. However, "they still did not know in what room the wounded person was located. A further message from dispatch said that there possibly was a rag or a T-shirt tied on the door handle to mark the room where the wounded teacher lay bleeding."[12] SWAT officers finally found the T-shirt they were looking for on a door near the scene of a large explosion. Shattered glass and bullets littered the floor. The SWAT officers who found Sanders called for immediate medical help and began evacuating the students from the room. Paramedics did not get to Sanders in time. He died at about 3:00 P.M., the only teacher to lose his life during the massacre at Columbine.

The identities of the other fourteen people found deceased at the scene—two outside, twelve in the school's library—would take many more hours to confirm. Because bodies are considered evidence in a crime scene, they must be left where they are while investigators process the scene. "Bodies should not be moved until the scene is photographed, the bodies photographed and tagged, and the location of the bodies charted, ideally on a grid pattern of the area,"[13] say medical examiners David Dolinak, Evan W. Matshes, and Emma O. Lew. Before the coroner could come in to identify and remove the bodies of the victims, the entire crime scene first had to be processed for evidence.

The task of processing the crime scene at Columbine was so formidable that it required organizing investigators into separate teams, each assigned to search and document an area of the large school. In addition to the complicated task of processing such a large crime scene, police had to find the evidence that would tell the story of what happened at the school that day. In the months and years that followed, the evidence they collected would be shown to the world, and they could not afford to overlook anything that might be important to the investigation. "The investigation should not be rushed," says Barry A. J. Fisher, the crime laboratory director for the Los Angeles County Sheriff's Department. "Others must wait. The investigator is personally responsible for his mistakes and has the right to determine personal actions at the scene."[14]

Small Sheriff's Office, Huge Task

The investigation of the Columbine High School shootings, one of the most notorious and complicated crimes scenes in American history, was a tremendous undertaking for the Jefferson County Sheriff's Office, a small force in a community that until then had been considered quiet, safe, and relatively crime free. Although the deputies who responded to the shootings at Columbine had never dealt with a murder scene of such scope and size, the job of the investigation was, at heart, no different than investigating any other crime that involves loss of life. "The purpose of the criminal investigation still remains first and foremost a search for truth," says crime scene analyst

The library forensic team focused on the room where most of the murders had taken place, which included destroyed computers and shot out windows.

Ross M. Gardner in his book, *Practical Crime Scene Processing and Investigation*. "The bottom line is that the police seek to objectively define what happened and who was involved."[15]

The Columbine Investigation Task Force, as the crime scene investigation team came to be called, had multiple teams of investigators, looking into different aspects of the crime. For processing the crime scene itself, there was an Outside Team that was assigned to the exterior of the school and that examined two cars the killers had rigged with explosives and left in the parking lot. The Cafeteria Team processed the lunchroom, where hundreds of students had been spending their lunch period when the shooting spree began and where the killers had deposited bombs large enough to have decimated much of the school. A third team, the Library Team, focused on processing the library, where most of the murders took place.

By breaking the crime scene down this way, investigators lessened the risk of missing any important evidence or information. "Mass crime scenes in many respects are no different than any other crime scene, at least in terms of the basic actions necessary to document and process them," says Gardner. "Zone searches" like the ones implemented at Columbine, he says, are "used effectively to subdivide a large crime scene into smaller, more manageable portions."[16] During zone searches of the school, investigators flagged pieces of evidence, everything from bullets and bullet casings to shrapnel from bombs. They looked for blood spatter and bullet holes. They looked for pipe bombs that had not yet detonated.

Team members from many different police jurisdictions helped the Jefferson County Sheriff's Office with processing the thousands of pieces of evidence that had to be collected and documented. In total, thirty-five different law-enforcement agencies, including the Federal Bureau of Investigation (FBI), the Bureau of Alcohol, Tobacco, Firearms and Explosives (ATF), and police departments from neighboring communities, took part in the investigation. Gardner says that the size and complexity of any mass murder scene like the one at Columbine "may stretch the capability of any single organization to handle the scene independently."[17] By relying on other jurisdictions for help, the Jefferson County Sheriff's Office ensured a faster and more thorough investigation of the crime scene.

Questions Loom

The goal of most crime scene investigations is to find evidence that identifies a suspect and evidence that a particular suspect committed the crime in question. At Columbine, where the two perpetrators had killed themselves in the library, the question of who did it was soon answered. Nevertheless, big questions remained: What was the time line of the events on that day? Where, when, and how had the killers moved through the school? Which killer shot each of the victims? A thorough investigation was the only way to answer these questions and to help Jefferson County and the nation take steps to prevent such a tragedy from happening again.

In deducing what exactly happened during the incident, investigators struggled to make sense of conflicting statements from hundreds of witnesses. Reports from confused bystanders had inaccurately convinced the SWAT teams that there had been as many as eight shooters inside the school, and such inaccurate reports continued to muddle the investigation once the shooting was over. "High levels of stress actually interfere with a person's ability to encode information," says Richard H. Walton, a former district attorney investigator in California and an expert in cold case homicides. "Memories are vulnerable to change by internal and external conditions, interactions with other persons, and exposure to additional information."[18] Most of the witnesses had been watching media coverage of the shootings and sharing information and stories with each other, activities that are known to affect how well people remember events. To determine what had really happened in the school during the rampage, investigators had to reconcile witnesses' statements with the actual evidence collected at the scene.

By combining information from witnesses and from evidence, investigators were eventually able to trace the path of the two gunmen through the school. Two important aspects of these determinations were blood-spatter analysis and ballistics. Blood-spatter analysis, the study of the direction and pattern in which blood sprays when a body is hit by something such as a bullet, helped determine where the victims were standing or sitting when they were injured. Ballistics, the study of how bullets are discharged from firearms and how they travel and impact the things they hit, indicated what type of firearms the shooters used and helped investigators determine where each gunman had been standing every time he fired a weapon. Each separate investigation team of the Columbine Investigation Task Force had blood-spatter analysts and ballistics experts to help them draw important conclusions about what exactly had happened in their assigned area of the school that day.

Blood Evidence

Blood-spatter evidence was critical in helping investigators figure out what happened every time one of the shooters pulled the trigger. "Spatter will assist in the location of the victim at the time of the discharge of the weapon . . . and assist with the reconstruction of the shooting,"[19] say bloodstain pattern analysts Stuart James, Paul Kish, and E. Paulette Sutton. The importance of blood patterns is "equal to that of fingerprints, shell casings, bullet holes, or murder weapons," says Louis L. Akin, a licensed professional investigator. "The interpretation of blood spatter patterns at crime scenes may reveal critically important information, such as the positions of the victim, assailant, and objects at the scene; the type of weapon used to cause the spatter; the minimum number of blows, shots, or stabs that occurred; and the movement and direction of the victim and assailant after bloodshed began."[20]

In cases of gunshot wounds, blood spatter indicates the direction the bullet came from. Because all the murder victims at Columbine were killed by gunfire, this kind of evidence was extremely important in processing the crime scene and figuring out where the gunmen and their victims had been at the moment each deadly shot was fired.

Blood-spatter evidence, such as the blood on this desk in the library, was critical for investigators to piece together what had happened.

Becoming a Forensic Firearms and Ballistics Analyst

Job Description
Forensic firearms and ballistics analysts participate in crime scene searches, help to reconstruct crimes, identify firearms and ammunition, and perform microscopic comparisons of bullets that have been fired from guns.

Education
Professionals in this field must have a four-year degree in forensic science and/or mechanical technology.

Qualifications
Firearms and ballistics analysts typically need two years of experience as a trainee in forensic firearms examination before they can pursue work in this field.

Additional Information
Firearms and ballistics analysts spend most of their time in a laboratory, although they sometimes respond to crime scenes to collect evidence. They occasionally are called to testify in court. They must be able to assemble and disassemble guns and have a working knowledge of every type of firearm and its ammunition.

Salary
$40,000 to $60,000 or more per year

What the blood-spatter evidence revealed in Columbine High School was disturbing. In the library, where ten of the thirteen murders happened, blood-spray patterns indicated that the killers shot their victims at close range. The killings had been callous and systematic. The victims had been crouching under tables, some with their hands over their faces. Some had been shot multiple times. This dreadful picture of the murder of defenseless victims was further supported by the ballistics experts, who analyzed the bullets the killers had used and the direction the bullets had come from.

Bullets in the Halls

Forensic ballistics experts study a bullet's journey through the barrel of a gun, through the air, and into the surface, body, or object with which it eventually collides. Investigators who specialize in ballistics also specialize in firearms and often are able to determine the type of gun (a pistol, for instance, or a shotgun or a rifle) that fired a bullet, just by looking at the bullet. Because every gun's barrel leaves unique marks on each bullet that travels through it, firearms examiners can tell which bullets passed through which gun by comparing the bullets collected at a crime scene. Forensic ballistics

Evidence tags mark bullet casings in the entryway to Columbine. A total of 329 shots were fired in and around the school.

experts also provide valuable insights about the shooter, the victim, and the circumstances surrounding a murder by gunfire.

"Interpretation of the violent and dynamic circumstances that have taken place within the crime scene is a necessary step in the reconstruction of events,"[21] says forensic ballistics expert Ian Prior. At Columbine, ballistics were as important as bloodspatter analysis in determining the sequence of the killers' actions. Every bullet is surrounded by a cartridge, or casing, that contains the explosives necessary to fire the bullet out of the gun when the trigger is pulled, so every time a gun fires, it ejects not only the bullet but the "spent" casing of the bullet. The casings along with the bullets themselves indicated where the shooters were standing every time a trigger was pulled. "From unfired cartridges at the scene," says Prior, ballistics investigators are also able to tell if a firearm malfunctioned or if "there was excitement on the offender's part, that a live round was worked through the action and ejected unintentionally."[22] Ballistics analysis helped investigators corroborate the reports of various eyewitnesses with the trail of spent and unfired bullet casings left throughout Columbine.

In all, the ballistics evidence collected by investigators at the crime scene showed that a total of 329 shots were fired in and around the high school that day. The killers fired 188 of these bullets. Law enforcement returned fire with 141 rounds of their own. Not all of the killers' bullets hit someone. Recorded 911 phone calls captured the sounds of the gunmen randomly shooting in the hallways, not aiming at anyone or anything in particular. Bullets were found lodged in walls and ceilings, and many seemed to have been fired just to make noise and terrify students. But the killers did murder thirteen people that day and injure two dozen more, and ballistics supported what the blood-spatter analysts found: Most of the victims were shot at close range.

Waiting for News

It took hours for investigators to conduct a thorough search for evidence and document what they found. Medical examiners had to wait until investigators were finished before any of the bodies at the scene could be moved. "Unless the ballistics expert and pathologist view the scene with the deceased *in situ*," says Prior (that is, with the bodies in their original positions), "then what is observed at the mortuary can become an unnecessary puzzle."[23] Only after reconstructing events based on where the bodies and evidence are lying can a time line of the events become clear. It was the next day before medical professionals could begin to handle the bodies and start to answer the one question the community was holding its breath to know: Who were the deceased?

During the evacuation of the school, families were sent to Leawood Elementary School, a quarter mile from Columbine High, to be reunited with the teenagers and teachers being rescued from the scene of the crime. Throughout the afternoon, everyone watched closely every time a new list of survivors' names arrived and was posted on the doors of the elementary school. Family members crowded around each new list, and many hugged each other and cried tears of relief. By that evening, almost all of Columbine High School's students and faculty members had been accounted for. Most were at home with their families. Some were at local hospitals, recovering from injuries or undergoing surgery to save their lives.

Now only a handful of families remained at the elementary school, anxiously waiting for news of their children. According to the *Denver Rocky Mountain News*, by the next morning "Jefferson County's district attorney held a list of 13 names— a teacher and 12 students who hadn't come home the night before." Jefferson County district attorney Dave Thomas did not want to wait any longer to tell the families what they already

Death of a Hero

On the day he died, William "Dave" Sanders had been a teacher and a coach at Columbine High for twenty-five years. On that horrible day, he never left his students, not even when gunfire erupted in the school lunchroom. Sanders urged students to run faster, up the stairs to the second floor. He stood at the top of the steps until every kid was hidden in classrooms, away from the gunmen. That was where Eric Harris shot Sanders, hitting him in the torso, the head, and the neck. Other teachers pulled Sanders into a classroom, and more than three hours passed as students took turns putting pressure on his wounds to slow the blood loss. Sanders died before paramedics reached him. He was the last person and the only teacher to die at Columbine that day. His family later sued the Jefferson County Sheriff's Office, stating that Sanders could have survived the shootings if rescue teams had reached him sooner. The county settled out of court with Sanders' family for $1.5 million.

suspected. "The teacher and the kids, Thomas knew in his heart, were dead."[24] While the families were quietly informed by the district attorney, it would be many more hours before investigators were through with crime scene procedure and ready to make any official announcements.

Coroners at Columbine

Nancy Bodelson, the Jefferson County coroner, was waiting outside the school for permission from investigators to go in and begin the work of examining and identifying the dead. "Each family had been asked to write down information about their child," says the official sheriff's report, "the age, hair and eye color, what the student wore to school that day, if she or he had obtained a driver's license, and any other characteristics that might help in the preliminary identification of the deceased."[25] Bodelson also looked through a Columbine High

School yearbook to find photographs of the students who were still missing. According to the sheriff's report, the command post had declared that "due to the continuing searches and safety concerns, no investigators would be allowed into the building until the following morning."[26] The investigators, the families, and the community would have to wait until the following day for confirmation of the names of the fifteen who had died at Columbine.

When Bodelson was finally allowed into the crime scene on Wednesday morning, she and a team of coroners examined the bodies in the positions where they lay, searching them for identification and matching their appearances with the yearbook photos and family descriptions. "The issue of identification in a disaster recovery effort is usually done by searching their body for ID, or using fingerprints,"[27] say criminalists Barry Fisher, David Fisher, and David Kolowski. Bodelson's team also collected fingerprints from the deceased.

Meanwhile, District Attorney Thomas made preliminary death notifications to the anxious families still waiting for news. "On Wednesday afternoon," says the official sheriff's

An evidence trailer outside Columbine. The police and coroners collected evidence from the deceased students to help identify them.

report, "they told each family that, based on current information obtained by the authorities, their child or spouse was likely among the fatalities."[28] On Wednesday night, a day and a half after the shootings, each victim was finally officially identified, most of them by the fingerprints filed when they had received their driving permits or driver licenses.

The official autopsies—medical examinations of deceased victims to determine the cause of death—took still another day. Four forensic pathologists were called in from neighboring counties to help examine the fifteen bodies recovered from Columbine and create the official reports on the exact injuries that resulted in each person's death. According to the official sheriff's report, "all the deaths were the result of gunshot wounds."[29] Two of the deaths, those of the gunmen, were determined to be suicides. By this time, at the homes of the gunmen, a second wave of intense investigation was already well under way—the investigation into the backgrounds of the killers who had carried out this bloody, tragic, and unforgettable attack.

CHAPTER 3

The Killers

Long before the smoke in Columbine High School began to clear, two names had surfaced from the testimonials of panicked students and teachers fleeing the school. As SWAT teams were entering Columbine to search for gunmen and survivors, investigators on the outside were taking witness statements from all who could provide them. Some officers interviewed evacuated students and staff on-site. Other officers were sent to area hospitals to talk to injured students. "Even as the events unfolded inside Columbine High School on April 20, 1999, investigators began their investigation of the shootings," says the official sheriff's report. "By noon, the majority of the Jefferson County Sheriff's Office investigators were on scene interviewing the fleeing students and faculty who provided vital information on what was occurring inside the school and who might be involved."[30]

It was soon evident that the individuals shooting guns and detonating bombs in the school were not anonymous, deranged strangers. They were a pair that Columbine High School already knew, two seniors who had spent the past four years walking the very halls in which they launched handmade bombs that day, seniors who had sat in classes with the very students on whom they decided to open fire. One of the teens had attended the senior prom three days earlier. Both were just weeks away from graduating and moving on with their lives. Their names were Dylan Klebold and Eric Harris.

The teens were known by the sheriff's office, too. Both already had criminal records. Even before the shootings were over, officers were sent to the Klebold and Harris homes to secure both residences while they waited for search warrants, the legal orders allowing law enforcement officers to search for and seize materials that may have been used to plan or commit a crime. Search warrants can be issued when police have reason to believe that a person is hiding evidence of a crime, items designed or intended to be used in a crime, or belongings the law does not permit him or her to possess. Multiple witnesses' claims that Dylan Klebold and Eric Harris were inside Columbine High School with guns and other weapons provided enough evidence to justify search warrants for their homes. "Searches of both suspects' residences were in progress before the bodies of the two killers were found inside the school,"[31] says the official sheriff's report. What investigators found inside the Klebold and Harris homes would bring up many questions about how two smart kids could turn so bad without anyone noticing.

Teens to Terrors

Eric Harris and Dylan Klebold had a lot in common. They loved computers and took computer programming classes together at Columbine, a subject at which they excelled. They played video games—their favorites were violent ones, especially a game called *Doom*. They listened to hard rock and were particularly fond of

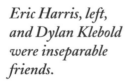

Eric Harris, left, and Dylan Klebold were inseparable friends.

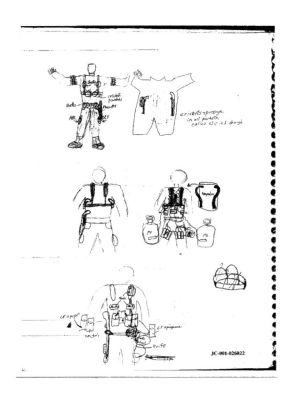

This drawing made by Eric Harris and Dylan Klebold showing where the weapons would be hidden on their bodies demonstrates how well-planned the attack was.

bands, such as KMFDM, Nine Inch Nails, and a German group called Rammstein. They worked together at Blackjack Pizza and bowled together at Belleview Lanes. They were intelligent, creative, and well spoken, although they did not care for most of their classes. Klebold loved theater and managed the sound for Columbine's school plays. Harris loved creating his own violent game levels in *Doom*. Harris was short, thin, and hot tempered. Klebold was tall, thin, and shy. They had few friends besides each other. By their sophomore year of high school, the two had become nearly inseparable. "We had all been one big group of friends," says former Columbine student Brooks Brown, describing how his relationship with Dylan and Eric changed during high school. "Now, though, Eric and Dylan were forming a bond that was much stronger than they had with the rest of us."[32]

Klebold and Harris each had an older brother who had already moved out of the family home. At the time of the shootings, each teen was the only kid still living with his parents. The Klebolds owned a large, expensive house built partly into a hillside of the

Rocky Mountains and surrounded by 10 acres (4ha) of land. The Harrises lived in a smaller, two-story suburban tract home with a small yard and a full basement that was Eric's private domain. The basement contained a bedroom, a living room, and Harris's computer. Like Klebold's room several miles away, Harris's basement space also harbored disturbing items. Investigators found explosives, ammunition, a coiled length of fuse for lighting bombs, personal journals, and a videotape the pair had made about what they were planning to do at Columbine.

As investigators combed through Klebold's and Harris's homes on the day of the shootings, they found enough evidence to link both teens to the murderous crime at Columbine. On the videotape made in Harris's basement in the weeks before the shootings, the two teens admitted to the crime they were about to commit in such detail that prosecuting the case might have turned out to be a fairly straightforward task. The boys essentially recorded their own confessions. "It will be the most nerve-racking 15 minutes of my life," Klebold told the video camera in Harris's basement. "After the bombs are set and we're waiting to charge through the school. Seconds will be like hours. I can't wait."[33]

However, there would be no day in court for Harris and Klebold. By the time their journals and videotapes were being collected from their rooms, the teens were already dead. Suicide had always been part of their plan, a plan they had been perfecting for more than a year. Harris, recording his thoughts on video, told the camera, "This is my last week on earth."[34] The day before the shootings, Klebold wrote in his diary, "In 26.4 hours I'll be dead, & in happiness."[35] The killers had never intended to come out of the school alive on the day of their attack.

Searching for Accomplices

By the time the massacre at Columbine High School was over, the Jefferson County Sheriff's Office was no longer trying to collect evidence to prove that Eric Harris and Dylan Klebold were guilty—the shooters had done that themselves through

Retrieving Computer Evidence

Important evidence in criminal cases often exists in a suspect's computer. Criminals may use computer programs to plan their crimes, make lists and diagrams, correspond with accomplices, do crime-related research, and even purchase materials they will use in the crime. Eric Harris's computer stored a great deal of information about the planning of and motivation for the shootings at Columbine. Listed below are the steps that crime scene specialists called forensic computer examiners take to retrieve and preserve information from suspects' computers.

1 The forensic computer examiner shuts down, disconnects, and transports the computer to a laboratory for examination.

2 The examiner immediately performs a system back up to protect the data against loss or damage.

3 The examiner then identifies all files on the system, including files that have been deleted but are still retrievable, as well as files that are encrypted or password protected.

4 If possible, the examiner restores files that have been deleted and retrieves information from hidden or encrypted files.

5 The examiner prints out relevant data and a list of all relevant files.

6 The examiner consults with police investigators on the findings, and if requested, provides computer-related testimony in court.

the materials they had left behind in their own bedrooms. Now investigators had to figure out how two teenagers managed to plan such an efficient and brutal operation and how they had come up with the murderous idea in the first place. According to sociologists and rampage shooting experts Glenn W. Muschert and Ralph W. Larkin, "those with military experience equated the Columbine attack with contemporary styles of urban warfare,"[36] a type of combat in which soldiers are trained to carry out military operations in buildings and public spaces filled with civilians. Investigators initially did not believe that Klebold and Harris, teenage boys with no formal military training, could have carried out such a well-planned, extensive attack without help. In the days following the killings, the investigation turned to a search for accomplices, people who had helped Harris and Klebold plan or prepare for the attack or even people who had known the attack was coming.

Investigators from the Jefferson County Sheriff's Office, with the help of many other agencies, including the FBI, began interviewing anyone who knew Harris and Klebold. These interviews, close to five hundred of them, took three days to complete. Through these interviews, investigators learned the names of all the friends and associates of Harris and Klebold. Then they searched for signs that any of these people had been involved in the crime.

The official sheriff's report says,

> The main objective of the investigation was to determine exactly what occurred at Columbine High School and to determine whether anyone else participated in the shootings, assisted in the planning or had prior knowledge of what Harris and Klebold did on April 20. Another objective was to interview every student, faculty member and employee of Columbine High School and determine where each individual was at the time of the shootings and what they witnessed.[37]

The work required about eighty investigators, who followed up on more than 4,400 leads. These interviews began to paint a disturbing picture of two withdrawn, angry friends who had become enthralled with violent music, movies, and video games and who were not afraid to break the law. In fact, the massacre at Columbine was not the first time the Jefferson County Sheriff's Office had heard of Eric Harris and Dylan Klebold.

Trouble with the Law

In January 1998, about fifteen months before their attack on Columbine, Harris and Klebold were arrested for breaking into a van and stealing $1,500 worth of electronics equipment. The Jefferson County District Attorney's office put the two young men into a diversion program for their crime. This program required that the teens perform community service, attend classes designed to raise their awareness of the consequences of their actions, write essays about their crime, and write apology letters to the owner of the van they broke into. Within a year's time, Klebold and Harris had worked hard in the program. They had convinced the diversion program's administrators that they were good kids who had done a stupid thing. Robert Kriegshauser, who oversaw Klebold's and Harris's cases, "had supervised maybe five hundred clients, although only ten to fifteen were 'exceptional,' and allowed to leave the program

Eric Harris had made death threats over the Internet towards Brooks Brown, a former friend and fellow Columbine student.

early," says journalist Jeff Kass in his book, *Columbine: A True Crime Story.* "Eric and Dylan were among that group."[38]

However, breaking into a vehicle and stealing its contents were not the only illegal activities that Klebold and Harris had been up to. While they were appearing to be exemplary participants in the diversion program, they were also building pipe bombs at home and detonating them in deserted outdoor spaces. For years, they also had been sneaking out at night to play pranks on people they disliked. "Eric had spray paint cans and superglue," says former Columbine student Brooks Brown, "and he told us how he and Dylan would sneak over to people's houses and vandalize them, because the person had said or done something at school."[39] Some of Harris and Klebold's pranks were violent, such as one Brown says they played on Halloween night of their junior year. "That night the two of them went up on the roof with a BB-gun and took shots at little kids who were trick-or-treating," Brown recalls. "They told us about this over lunch, laughing like it was the funniest joke in the world."[40] The teens also drank alcohol from stashes they had hidden in their rooms. Dylan Klebold's nickname was VoDKa, after his favorite alcoholic drink. He capitalized his initials, DK, in the word.

The Jefferson County Sheriff's Office had other allegations on file that related to Eric Harris in particular—death threats he had been making on his personal Web site. Among the people Harris mentioned he wanted to kill was Brown, a childhood friend of Klebold and a former friend of Harris. Brown and Harris had a falling out, and then Harris began to mention Brown's name in his violent Internet musings. "It didn't take much anymore to set Eric off,"[41] Brown said. After a fight the

two had about Brown driving Harris to school in the mornings, Harris grew angry and wrote things on his Web site about Brown. "All I want to do is kill and injure as many of you as I can," Harris wrote, "especially a few people. Like Brooks Brown."[42]

Shocked and frightened by the angry content of Harris's Web site, the Brown family reported it to the Jefferson County Sheriff's Office. More than once, the Browns followed up on their report to see what, if anything, had been done about Harris's threats. Jefferson County investigator Mike Guerra was assigned to the case. He tried to get a search warrant, at one point, so he could seize the teen's computer, but the warrant was never approved, because the threats alone were not enough evidence that Harris had actually committed any crime to justify a warrant. The Browns had also asked the police to remain anonymous because

Eric Harris, left, and Dylan Klebold hold guns in a video that was part of a school project. The two got in trouble for having guns in their senior class picture.

By the Numbers

7 1/2

Minutes duration of the killing spree in the Columbine library, where the gunmen killed ten students and wounded twelve others.

they feared Harris would lash out at them in revenge if he knew they had reported him. Therefore, no formal charges were pressed. Police officers never went to Harris's home or spoke with him or his parents about the Web site, not even after Brown and his parents printed out the Web pages and gave them to police. The Web site explained in detail much of Harris and Klebold's plan for Columbine, but it was still up on the Internet the day the shootings took place.

Trouble at School

Klebold and Harris also had problems at school prior to the shootings. The two were suspended for hacking into the school's database of locker combinations and breaking into the lockers of several fellow students. Klebold later received another suspension for vandalizing the locker of a student who had angered him. The pair also raised concern among teachers for making violent films and writing violent essays. One of Klebold's creative writing papers was so violent, in fact, that Columbine teacher Judith Kelly called it "the most vicious story I have ever read."[43] A senior-class picture taken for the yearbook shortly before the shootings shows Klebold and Harris aiming fake guns at the camera. Harris was also taking antidepressant medication prescribed to control his mood swings and obsessive-compulsive traits. Looking back, critics of the school and the sheriff's office claim that warning signs of violence were obvious and that school administrators and deputies either missed the clues or ignored them. However, aside from causing minor trouble such as locker vandalism, Harris and Klebold never particularly worried most of their peers at Columbine. "In a school of 1,800 students, Eric did not stand out," says Larkin. "He and Dylan were able to keep their plans

concealed from their closest associates."[44] Although Harris's and Klebold's parents knew about their sons' 1998 arrest, they seemed to trust the officials who released the teens from the diversion program early for exemplary behavior. According to the people who knew them, Harris and Klebold seemed to be preparing for life after high school. Klebold had been accepted at the University of Arizona and took a road trip with his parents the month before the attack to pick out his dorm room there. Harris met with a Marine Corps recruiter, showing interest in a military career like his father's. To everyone around them, Harris and Klebold appeared to be planning for life after graduation, just like the rest of their classmates.

Harris, left, and Klebold practice shooting at a rifle range in the long black trench coats they wore as part of the Trenchcoat Mafia.

It was actually just a terrible ruse. The teenagers fed lies to those around them while they fed their own anger and hatred for their high school and everyone in it. "I could convince them that I'm going to climb Mount Everest, or I have a twin brother

Prescription for Disaster?

Gunman Eric Harris had been taking Luvox, a prescription medication that helps with depression and obsessive-compulsive disorder—a chronic state of anxiety and unwanted, recurring thoughts and feelings. The medication was supposed to help Harris overcome the very kinds of violent thoughts he acted on during his shooting rampage. In fact, in some of the journals and videotapes Harris and Klebold left behind, Harris mentions he planned to stop taking the medication so that his rage could build. (Sudden withdrawal from antidepressant medication can cause aggressive thoughts and behavior.)

Harris's autopsy revealed he had a low level of Luvox in his system on the day of the shootings, and this led some of the victims' families to file a lawsuit against the company that makes Luvox, claiming that the medication may have impaired Harris's reasoning and been a factor in the attack. In 2004, five years after Columbine, the U.S. Food and Drug Administration issued a report that antidepressant medication can, in fact, worsen depression and suicidal thoughts in teenagers, but in 1999, doctors were not yet aware of this danger. The level of the drug in Harris's system during his autopsy were consistent with the therapeutic dose he was prescribed, and it is possible that he was using the medication normally at the time of the massacre. It is also possible that he had been taking higher doses on purpose before the attack, then stopped taking the drug altogether to worsen his aggression, resulting in a dwindling level of the drug that remained in his system on the day he died.

The autopsy report could not confirm which scenario was the truth. In any case, the medication cannot be blamed for giving Harris his aggressive ideas in the first place. Investigators discovered violent entries in Harris's journal that were written long before he began taking Luvox, and Harris's use of Luvox did not explain how Klebold, who was not taking the drug, could also be so violent. Like many of the issues surrounding the massacre at Columbine, the actual role Luvox had in the disaster remains a mystery. The victims' families eventually dropped the lawsuit against the drug's manufacturer.

growing out of my back," Eric said to his video camera a month before the shootings. "I can make you believe anything."[45] On April 20, to the horror of a school, a community, and a nation, Harris and Klebold proved they had covered up their plans so well that no one, not even their parents, suspected what they were about to do.

The Trenchcoat Mafia

Even after seizing computers, journals, and videotapes in which Harris and Klebold repeatedly insisted they would be committing the crime alone, investigators were reluctant to accept that the two young men had been able to keep a secret that huge and pull off a crime that large without help. Investigators looked into Harris's and Klebold's hobbies and interests for clues that might lead them to acquaintances who knew one or both of the killers and who might have had a role in the crime. The investigators' quest to learn more inevitably came down to questions about the computer games Harris and Klebold played, the

The main page from the Trenchcoat Mafia Web site.

music they listened to, the people they hung out with (a very small percentage of the students at Columbine), and perhaps most significantly, one item of clothing that the teens liked to wear—black trench coats, the favored dress of a social group at Columbine that was called the Trenchcoat Mafia.

The name *Trenchcoat Mafia* itself implies violence and crime, and the students who belonged to it—social outcasts, by their own description—dressed weird, listened to loud music, and acted mysteriously enough to make investigators suspect they may have been involved in the massacre. "Early intelligence information gathered at the crime scene from witnesses referred to Harris and Klebold's involvement, or membership, in a group at Columbine High School commonly known as the Trenchcoat Mafia (TCM),"[46] says the official sheriff's report. All members and associates of the TCM "were to be interviewed and investigated by the associates team," the report says. "The goal was to determine if any other person may have participated or conspired with Harris and Klebold in the preparation or carrying out of the events of April 20 or any related crime" and "to identify anyone who had any prior knowledge that Harris and Klebold were planning the shootings."[47]

Two days after the massacre, journalists Susan Greene and Bill Briggs wrote in the *Denver Post*, "Classmates describe the shooting suspects as part of a clique of generally quiet, brooding students with penchants for dark trench coats, all-black clothes and shaved heads. By several accounts, the group [is] also interested in the occult, mutilation, shock-rocker Marilyn Manson and Adolf Hitler."[48]

Like Harris and Klebold, members of the TCM considered themselves nonconformists. They were questioned extensively by investigators about how well they knew Harris and Klebold and what they knew about the shootings. The connection between TCM and the shooters, however, was not as strong as it appeared at first to investigators. In fact, Harris and Klebold had not officially belonged to the group at all. "The Trenchcoat Mafia was a loose, social affiliation of former and current Columbine High School students with no formal organizational structure,

Trenchcoat Mania

In the aftermath of the massacre at Columbine, one article of clothing emerged as a nationwide symbol of school shooters: The trench coats Dylan Klebold and Eric Harris wore during the attack. The coats were more of a practical choice than anything—they covered up the guns and explosives the teens had strapped to their bodies. But the media latched onto stories about a group they claimed was headed by Harris and Klebold—the Trenchcoat Mafia. The myth grew, and some people began to believe the Trenchcoat Mafia had chapters in other high schools, planning similar rampages. Teens in trench coats now stood for terror. School dress codes began banning the coats.

In reality, although there had been a group at Columbine called the Trenchcoat Mafia, Harris and Klebold were not part of it. Despite some students' claims that the killers belonged to the group, a yearbook picture of the Trenchcoat Mafia taken the year before the shootings does not include Harris or Klebold, and the caption mentions playing foosball, not planning murder. Investigators ruled out any connection between the group and the killers. The trench coat myth, however, lived on.

leadership or purpose,"[49] says the official sheriff's report. Most of the original TCM members had graduated the year before the shootings, and those who were still around at the time of the shootings did not consider Harris and Klebold close friends.

Despite the way news reporters initially presented it, the TCM was not a dangerous gang within Columbine. Investigators eventually concluded the group had nothing to do with the shooting.

The Killers Acted Alone

Investigators identified twenty-two people considered to be friends of the killers who perhaps could have known something about what was going to happen. Investigators questioned these twenty-two individuals, searched their property, and confiscated thirteen of their personal computers, looking for documents or other clues that Harris and Klebold had help in planning their attacks. None of the thirteen computers or any of the interviews gave police any evidence that Harris and Klebold had ever shared their plans with anyone.

In the end, investigators determined that Harris and Klebold planned and carried out their crime much the same way they died in the library that day—through their own will, in their own way, and by their own hands. "The Columbine Task Force investigation concluded that evidence indicates that no one, other than Eric Harris and Dylan Klebold, participated in the shootings at Columbine High School on April 20, 1999," says the official sheriff's report. "Additionally, there is no known evidence that anyone, other than Harris and Klebold, assisted in the planning or had any prior knowledge of that plan."[50]

One question—who was responsible for the massacre—had been answered. But the investigation was far from over. Two big questions still loomed—how the pair had pulled off their crime and perhaps more importantly, why.

CHAPTER 4

The Weapons

In the state of Colorado, it is illegal for someone younger than eighteen to buy or own guns. It is also illegal for anyone to possess certain "dangerous" weapons, which include machine guns, shortened shotguns, and shortened rifles. Anyone who owns one of these dangerous weapons commits a class-five felony, which is punishable by one to three years in prison and a fine of between fifty thousand dollars and a hundred thousand dollars. Unknown to almost everyone but themselves, Harris and Klebold were class-five felons long before they murdered thirteen people. They possessed multiple weapons classified as "dangerous" by the state of Colorado, and they could have been sent to prison for simply owning them. How they were able to obtain the weapons and why they were never caught with the guns before they used them against their classmates came under scrutiny in the aftermath of the shooting.

Investigators also searched for a motive. Why did these teenagers carry out such a horrific act? They learned that Eric Harris was fascinated with killing people. He wrote about it often in his journal and on his Web site. He believed in naturalist Charles Darwin's biological theory of natural selection, which states that only the strongest and most capable individuals of a species will survive and that nature eliminates weakness. Harris applied this theory to people as well. He thought of himself as superior to other people and felt that few others were worthy of surviving. "I feel like God," he wrote in a journal that investigators later took from his home. "I am higher than almost anyone . . . in terms of universal intelligence."[51] Harris's feelings of superiority may have been the main reason for his murderous crime. The T-shirt he wore on the day of the shootings read, "Natural Selection." And although Dylan Klebold did not worship Charles Darwin the way Harris did, he did seem to worship Harris. When it came to collecting bombs and guns and fantasizing about killing people, Klebold played along.

The Killers' Firearms

When investigators processed the school library, they discovered that Harris and Klebold had each carried two guns. Harris had a 9-millimeter carbine rifle and a 12-gauge shotgun. Klebold also carried a 12-gauge shotgun, plus a semiautomatic handgun called a TEC-DC9, a gun that, according to an article in the *Denver Post*, "has figured in several high profile crimes and is favored by street gangs ... [it] bears a menacing resemblance to a machine pistol."[52] In addition, both shotguns had their barrels cut down, meaning the end of the barrels had been sawed off. Sawed-off shotguns are prohibited weapons in Colorado. "Sawing off a shotgun, a federal crime, allows the buckshot to disperse across a wider area and do more damage,"[53] said the article in the *Denver Post*. When Harris's home was searched on the day of the shootings, investigators found the portion of the shotgun barrel that he had sawed off.

A video shows Eric Harris and Dylan Klebold shooting in the cafeteria during their rampage in Columbine High School.

Tracing a Gun

Gun manufacturers engrave every gun with a serial number, and every legal gun sale creates a record of the seller and the buyer, creating a trail of ownership for every firearm. The Bureau of Alcohol, Tobacco, Firearms and Explosives (ATF) keeps a database of all guns bought and sold in the United States. When a gun is found at a crime scene, the ATF can use the serial number to trace the gun to the manufacturer, which in turn can name the retailer that sold the gun. A gun can sometimes be traced directly to the person who used it in the crime. If a gun used in a crime was stolen or bought illegally, any legal sale of the gun during its lifetime can still give investigators important leads for tracking down suspects.

Many criminals think that destroying the serial number on a gun will make it untraceable. However, police laboratories have ways to restore damaged serial numbers, making it nearly impossible to prevent a gun from being traced. The TEC-DC9 handgun used in the shootings at Columbine still had a serial number and would have been easy to trace to Mark Manes, the man who illegally sold the gun to the killers. Manes saved the police the trouble. He turned himself in.

One of the videotapes found in the killers' homes also showed the gunmen practicing with their weapons in the weeks before the attack. "Both are shooting their sawed-off shotguns," says the official sheriff's report. "It seems clear that they're still getting used to them. Their hands are bleeding because they've sawed off so much of the gun. The recoil from the weapons is substantial—and quite painful for a gunman to shoot repeatedly."[54]

It was important for investigators to figure out how the killers had obtained their guns. They knew that the teens would have faced two obstacles in getting this firepower. First, they would need enough cash to purchase the weapons, and second, they would need someone eighteen years old or older to buy the guns for them since eighteen is the minimum age for buying a rifle or shotgun in the state of Colorado. Investigators discovered that Harris and Klebold had saved their wages from their part-time jobs. Harris earned about seven dollars an hour working at Blackjack Pizza. Klebold earned just over five dollars an hour. The two saved enough money to pay for all four of their firearms in cash. Once they had the funds, however, they were still too young to buy the guns themselves. Investigators knew someone had to have helped Harris and Klebold purchase their weapons.

Mark Manes was sentenced to six years in jail for supplying the TEC-DC9 pistol that Harris and Klebold used in the Columbine killings.

Buying the Guns

Investigators learned who helped Harris and Klebold acquire their weapons from the killers' own diaries and videotapes. One of the helpers was Klebold's friend Robyn Anderson, who had been eighteen for about two weeks when Harris and Klebold asked her to help them buy three of the four guns they would eventually use in the massacre. The boys told her they

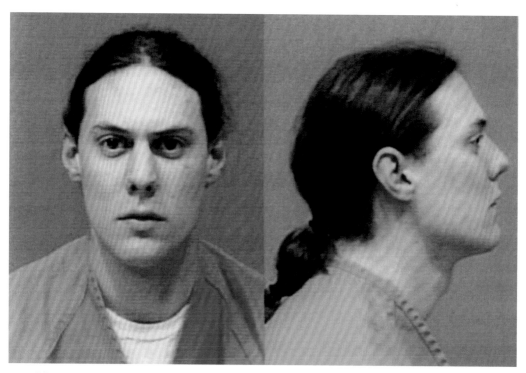

wanted a few guns in order to go hunting. She accompanied them to the Tanner Gun Show in Denver and presented her ID to the gun sellers, proving she was of legal age to purchase the weapons. Harris and Klebold paid the gun sellers themselves, in cash. There were no receipts for their purchases, but the killers did leave an evidence trail in their journals when they chronicled their path to gun ownership. The day the first three guns were purchased, Harris wrote, "Well folks, today was a very important day. We have GUNS! It's all over now."[55] Harris and Klebold set to work sawing off the barrels of their guns, making them suitable for a far deadlier purpose than target shooting or hunting. They later mentioned Anderson by name in a video they recorded in Harris's basement shortly before the shootings: "Thanks to the gun show, and to Robyn,"[56] they told the camera.

The fourth firearm used in the massacre, the TEC-DC9 assault handgun Klebold carried, proved more difficult for Harris and Klebold to purchase. Not only is it illegal for a firearms dealer in the United States to sell any handgun to someone younger than twenty-one, but the TEC-DC9 is also in a class of handguns that is prohibited by the Federal Assault Weapons Ban of 1994, making it a rare weapon to find. Harris and Klebold tracked down the TEC-DC9 when twenty-two-year-old Philip Duran, one of their coworkers at Blackjack Pizza, introduced them to Mark Manes, a twenty-one-year-old man who owned the kind of handgun they said they wanted. Manes later told investigators he had known the teens were not old enough to legally own the weapon, but he sold his TEC-DC9 to them anyway, charging them five hundred dollars for the gun. Agents from the Bureau of Alcohol, Tobacco, Firearms and Explosives (ATF) initially linked Manes to the illegal sale of the gun because he appeared on a video Klebold and Harris made of their "target practice." In the video, Manes was shooting a sawed-off shotgun of his own (the possession of which is a felony in Colorado). Klebold also mentions Manes by name in a video recorded in Harris's basement: "Oh, and I'd like to make a thank you to Mark [Manes] and Phil [Duran]. Very cool. You helped us do what we needed to do."[57]

Even without the killers' own videos admitting how they had purchased an assault handgun, the ATF would have been able to identify Manes. "The Bureau of Alcohol, Tobacco and Firearms traced the TEC-DC9, found its last owner and that led them to Manes,"[58] reported the *Denver Rocky Mountain News*. ATF agents arrested Manes for selling a semiautomatic pistol to underage buyers. Even though he also purchased ammunition for Harris the day before the shootings, Manes insisted he had no idea why Harris and Klebold wanted the gun and the bullets. He received six years in prison anyway. Duran, the man who had introduced Harris and Klebold to Manes, owned a sawed-off shotgun himself. He received four and a half years in prison for that and for his role in supplying the teens with one of their weapons.

Duran and Manes were the only two people who served time in prison. Robyn Anderson was never arrested or charged with a crime. Because she purchased the guns legally and from legal gun sellers, she did not break any laws.

The Rest of the Arsenal

In addition to the four guns, none of which Harris and Klebold had been old enough to purchase and two of which were modified so they would be illegal for anyone to own, the killers carried an array

Along with the several knives, pipe bombs, and guns that Harris and Klebold had with them in the school, numerous makeshift bombs and guns were found in Eric Harris's car.

HARRIS
VEHICLE

of knives with them into the school on the day of their rampage. They did not use their knives to harm anyone. They did, however, make plentiful use of the third element of their deadly arsenal—explosives they had made mostly from materials readily available at hardware stores, using instructions they had found on the Internet and that Harris recreated on his own Web site.

As soon as the attack on Columbine was underway, sheriff's deputies knew that the killers had bombs. One officer, Deputy Magor, had responded to a pipe bomb in a field 3 miles (4.8km) from Columbine High School just moments before the attacks began. Harris and Klebold had planted the bomb earlier that morning to draw law enforcement's attention away from the real crime the teens were going to carry out. Altogether, there were 357 pieces of physical evidence related to explosives found within Columbine High School after the rampage. Harris and Klebold had detonated thirty of their self-made bombs before killing themselves. When their bodies were found, the pockets of their cargo pants were stuffed with explosives. Dozens more bombs were later found in the school, all of which had to be removed by bomb squads before investigators could safely move around inside the building. Parked outside in the school parking lot, Klebold's car contained another twelve bombs, and Harris's car had one bomb inside. The killers apparently had intended for their cars to explode and injure emergency personnel in the parking lot. When investigators searched the boys' homes, they found six additional bombs in Klebold's bedroom and two in Harris's bedroom. In total, Harris and Klebold had constructed ninety-nine explosives.

Harris and Klebold seemed to like bombs even more than guns. Harris, in particular, wrote a great deal about explosives in his journals. "I want to torch and level everything,"[59] he wrote. One type of bomb the teens made was a pipe bomb. Fashioned out of a length of pipe filled with an explosive substance, a pipe

By the Numbers

700

Number of student backpacks at Columbine that investigators had to search for explosives

Bomb Squads

A bomb squad is a group of technicians trained to handle explosives. Their job is to remove or disable bombs. Bomb technicians wear special suits and helmets to protect them if a bomb explodes while they are near it. The suits shield the technicians from a blast and cushion their fall if an explosion knocks them off their feet. Many bomb squads also use robots to carry explosives to a bomb truck or trailer, which has a series of pressure-release valves so that if a bomb explodes inside, the force of the explosion is contained and slowly released without hurting anyone.

Sixteen certified bomb technicians worked the crime scene at Columbine High School. They wore protective suits and transported the bombs they found in the school to a bomb trailer outside. While one of the technicians was lowering a bomb into the bomb trailer, it exploded, setting off other bombs that were already in the trailer. Because the bomb technicians were wearing protective suits, no one was injured, but it is a testament to how dangerous Harris and Klebold's explosives were.

bomb bursts with enormous pressure when its fuse is lit. Bomb technicians found pipe bombs of various sizes throughout the school. Harris and Klebold also made bombs out of carbon dioxide cartridges. Like the pipe bombs, the carbon dioxide explosives did considerable damage to the school. But they were mere accessories to two monstrous bombs that Harris and Klebold had stowed in the school cafeteria shortly after 11 A.M., right before their massacre began. Although these bombs never detonated, they had the explosive power to destroy much of the school and take many more lives than the killers' guns could.

An Explosive Failure

When the ATF agents investigating the shootings at Columbine took a close look at what Harris and Klebold had brought into the school for their rampage, they came to a startling conclusion: The massacre did not happen exactly as Harris and Klebold had planned. The killers had meant for their explosives to cause much more devastation than the bombs actually did. All the murder victims were killed by bullets, but the size and explosive potential of the two largest bombs revealed that Harris and Klebold had intended for their bombs to be the major source of damage. They had not been planning a shooting that day. They had been planning an explosion that would kill hundreds of people.

The killers' journals and other writings supported this conclusion. Investigators discovered diagrams of the school cafeteria and a time line of events as Klebold and Harris expected them to unfold. "Klebold's last entry in his school notebook gave a chilling timeline for April 20," says the official sheriff's report. "'Walk in, set bombs at 11:09 for 11:17. Leave.'" Klebold and Harris planned to wait outside for the explosion. "The belief is that they then would shoot any surviving students who were able to escape the fireball,"[60] says the report.

On the day of their rampage, Harris and Klebold lugged duffel bags into the cafeteria, heavy parcels that each hid a 20-pound (9kg) propane tank fashioned into a bomb, equipped with a timer and set to explode at exactly 11:17 A.M. "Because of faulty wiring and poorly constructed devices, the two 20-lb. propane bombs did not detonate,"[61] says the official sheriff's report. If the tanks had exploded as Harris and Klebold

The bombs set around the school were poorly made and most did not detonate, preventing the death toll from being much higher.

intended, the massacre would have been known not as the worst school shooting in the history of the United States, but the worst domestic terrorist bombing the country had ever seen. Hundreds of students and teachers would have died in the blast.

"The explosion of the two propane bombs could turn just about anything into shrapnel," says hazardous materials expert John R. Cashman. "A giant fireball would suck up oxygen, making death welcome to many victims and ensuring that survival was all but impossible." According to Cashman, "if Klebold and Harris had a better understanding of explosive reactions, electrical wiring, and current,"[62] then the death toll at Columbine would have dwarfed the 168 deaths in the 1995 bombing of the Alfred P. Murrah Federal Building in Oklahoma City, Oklahoma.

A View of the Bombs

The school's cafeteria was equipped with surveillance cameras that recorded part of the lunch period that day, and the duffel bags are visible in tapes. Harris and Klebold are visible as well when they walked down the stairs in the midst of their attack, heading through a now vacant lunchroom and shooting at the propane tank bombs that had malfunctioned. They even tossed smaller bombs at one of the bigger ones, trying to make it explode. A fiery flash is visible on the surveillance tape, but the school's fire sprinkler system was activated, quickly putting out the flame. "The propane tank was impervious," says author Dave Cullen in his book, *Columbine*. "The boys had been going for an inferno; they caused a flood."[63]

Jeff Britegam, one of the bomb squad members who responded to the scene, told the *Denver Post* that Klebold and Harris "had some right stuff to do a lot of destruction, but they just didn't know how to build them. You could look at a device and know they weren't experts, although it did take a lot of time for them to build all the devices. They didn't know 100 percent what they were doing—and that was a very good thing."[64]

A Preventable Tragedy?

Harris and Klebold stated in their videotapes that there was nothing any law or regulation could have done to prevent their crime. Harris told his video camera that if they hadn't gotten the guns the way they did, "we would have found something else."[65] *TIME* magazine reporters say there were many opportunities for Harris and Klebold to get caught. "They 'came close' one day, when an employee of Green Mountain Guns called Harris' house and his father answered the phone," the article says. "'Hey, your clips [devices that hold bullets for handguns] are in,' the clerk said. His father replied that he hadn't ordered any clips."[66] Apparently, Harris's father never asked if the clerk was calling the right phone number, and the clerk never pressed the issue. Just one question could have alerted the Harrises and the ammunition store that an underage teen was buying bullets for a handgun. Other such questions asked along the way might have been enough to expose Harris and Klebold's intentions and prevent the massacre.

As the investigation drew to a close, the community and the rest of the nation accepted what happened at Columbine. Attention eventually shifted from what could have prevented the massacre to what might prevent school shootings in the future. People started looking deeper into the shooting at Columbine, trying to answer the one question that the evidence had not: Why did they do it? If it can be learned why Eric Harris and Dylan Klebold planned and carried out a deadly assault on their school, then parents, schools, law enforcement, and communities can learn to identify and respond to kids like Harris and Klebold—not just during an attack, but before one can occur.

CHAPTER 5

Lessons Learned

In April 1999 a month before their high school graduation, most of Columbine's seniors were dreaming of colleges and careers. Eric Harris and Dylan Klebold had their sights set on the future, too—particularly on exiting the world as notorious killers. In their journals and their videotapes, they tallied up the body count they were hoping for. For at least a year before they walked into their high school loaded down with guns and bombs, they knew they would not be walking across a stage in a cap and gown to accept a diploma, and if they had their way, neither would hundreds of their classmates.

At the end of their junior year, Klebold wrote in Harris's yearbook how he was looking forward to "the holy April morning of NBK," referring to "Natural Born Killers," the pair's code name for the attack they had planned. "Killing enemies, blowing up stuff, killing cops!!"[67] Klebold wrote. Harris later drew Xs or wrote death threats over most of the faces in his junior yearbook. The two teenagers spent their senior year of high school planning a rampage that they hoped would keep them in the news for years to come. "I have a goal to destroy as much as possible,"[68] Harris wrote in his journal.

They did not pull off their self-professed day of glory exactly as they had planned. Harris and Klebold would probably have been disappointed to learn that they had killed only thirteen people and wounded twenty-three others, far fewer than the hundreds of deaths they intended to cause. Nevertheless, they did get one of their wishes: fame. The names of Eric Harris and Dylan Klebold have gone down in history as the perpetrators of the worst school shooting that had ever taken place in the nation as of 1999. But the two students looking

This drawing by Harris and Klebold shows the violent thoughts of the two killers.

for fame that day would never know that in the years after their rampage, their shooting spree did not spark the violent, nationwide school revolt they wrote about in their journals. What it did was change the way schools and law enforcement react to a gunman on a school campus, making it much less likely that someone will be able to repeat the massacre that happened at Columbine.

No Time to Wait

When 911 calls began pouring in to Jefferson County Sheriff's dispatch on the morning of April 20, 1999, every deputy in the area sped to the campus. Within moments, sheriff's cruisers were descending on the school parking lot from every direction, and the school was quickly surrounded. For the next forty-five minutes, while gunfire could be heard inside the school, deputies did nothing more. Procedure at the time required deputies to wait for SWAT teams to arrive.

While deputies waited outside, Klebold and Harris had the better part of an hour in which they had the school to themselves. "Half a dozen cops arrived every minute," writes Cullen.

"Nobody seemed to be in charge. Some cops wanted to assault the building, but that was not the plan." What they did instead was follow their training. Cullen says, "they reinforced the perimeter."[69]

Remembering the Victims

In the weeks immediately following the massacre at Columbine, Greg Zanis, a carpenter from Illinois who travels the country erecting "Crosses for Losses" at the sites of tragic events, placed fifteen wooden crosses into a hillside overlooking Columbine High School as a tribute to those who died in the school that day—including Eric Harris and Dylan Klebold. Each cross was labeled with a name and had a pen attached so mourners visiting the memorial could write their thoughts about the person.

The fifteen wooden "Crosses for Losses" that were erected soon after the shootings at Columbine. Black plastic was draped over Dylan Klebold's and Eric Harris's crosses by an anonymous mourner.

There were 125,000 visitors to the memorial site in its first few days. There was controversy, too, about whether there should be crosses for the two killers alongside the crosses for their victims. Brian Rohrbough, father of victim Daniel Rohrbough, eventually tore down the crosses for Harris and Klebold.

In September 2007, a permanent, official memorial of the tragedy was completed and dedicated in Clement Park, which adjoins the campus of Columbine High School. An acre in size and fashioned with Colorado stone that has been etched with sayings from the community, the new memorial is a peaceful place for people to remember the lives lost at Columbine High School.

In the days and weeks after the shootings, parents of victims demanded to know why police did not act more quickly on that day. "The majority of killings occurred at Columbine while the first responding officers were right outside the building," says David B. Stein a psychology professor at Longwood University in Virginia and a consultant to the Virginia State Police. They were waiting for the nearest SWAT team to arrive, he says, "which it did well below average response times."[70] But according to Stein, traditional police procedure may have resulted in loss of lives. He says "it has become evident that law enforcement needs to rethink old ways and take a completely new and progressive approach"[71] to situations such as school shootings.

A New Kind of Killer

The shootings at Columbine High School made law enforcement agencies around the country review their procedures. Officers who responded to Columbine expected the killers to try to escape or to exchange hostages for something they wanted. Traditionally, going into a school under those circumstances can make the shooters panic and kill more people. But Harris and Klebold were not like the killers that law enforcement had

Neither Harris nor Klebold planned on getting out of the school alive that day.

been trained to handle. The two teens were suicidal killers. They were not interested in taking hostages or negotiating with law enforcement, and they never had any intention of getting out of the school alive that day. Their one motivation was to hurt as many people as they could before taking their own lives.

In the wake of that violent day at Columbine, many law enforcement agencies around the country changed the way they respond to a gunman in a school or other crowded public place. The first officers to respond to such a scene no longer wait for backup. Now they are trained in rapid response.

Rapid Response

Journalist Darcia Harris Bowman of *Education Week* magazine describes rapid response as "a police tactic aimed at apprehending armed suspects in crowded buildings such as schools as quickly as possible." She says that Klebold and Harris "changed the rules when they descended on Columbine High School … now, many experts believe police can no longer afford to wait."[72] The rapid-response tactics in which law enforcement is now trained mean it is much less likely that gunmen such as Harris and Klebold would have the better part of an hour to kill freely. Officers are now trained to storm a building as soon as they arrive at a scene where active shooters are present.

Not everyone agrees that rapid-response tactics are the best way to handle an active shooter in a school. In fact, many law enforcement departments around the country praised the way the Jefferson County Sheriff's Office handled the chaos at Columbine, even though it did not use rapid-response techniques. "Quickness is no substitute for caution in the face of potential violence,"[73] one police officer told *Education Week*. But Ronald D. Stephens, executive director of the National School Safety Center, said that "the older command-and-control technique is no match for the video-game-style gun violence some of the nation's schools have seen." The shootings at Columbine, he said, "placed school and police officials on notice that this is the way these crises would unfold on campus … the bottom line is, this is a different approach for a different time."[74] In the years since the massacre at Columbine, would-be school shooters now face an immediate response from police who are prepared to chase killers into a building and use deadly force to stop an assault.

No Excuse for Negligence

Law enforcement procedure was not the only thing that began to change in America following the shootings at Columbine. Multiple lawsuits were filed in the Jefferson County courts in an effort to hold various parties accountable for their role in what Harris and Klebold did and to set legal standards that could be used in court cases in the future. The families of some of the victims sued the sheriff's office for its seemingly delayed response to the shootings. Several families also filed lawsuits against Klebold's and Harris's parents, seeking compensation for murders and serious injuries that they believed could have been prevented if the parents had just looked in their sons' bedrooms, where guns, knives, and bombs had been hidden long before the attack.

Doom was Harris's favorite video game. Lawsuits filed against the makers of the game stated that it may have trained Harris in some of the military tactics he used in the killings.

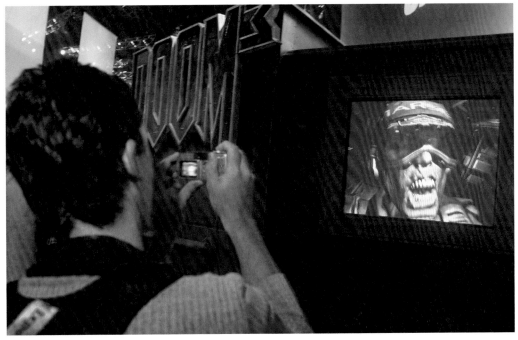

Lawsuits were also filed against the makers of the violent movies that Klebold and Harris watched and against the company that manufactured the video game *Doom*, which had been Harris's favorite. Some said the game may have taught Harris some of the military tactics he used against his classmates at Columbine. Still other victims blamed bands that played the edgy rock music Klebold and Harris listened to, such as KMFDM and Rammstein. J. D. Tanner, who organized the Tanner Gun Show where the killers obtained three of their four guns, was also named in a lawsuit by the families of victims.

Most of these lawsuits were thrown out before they got to court. A judge ruled that there was not enough evidence to prove that the accused parties had broken any laws, had acted with any criminal intent, or had any knowledge of a criminal act. But the cases still stirred up intense controversy about whether the lawsuits contradicted two important constitutional amendments. Defenders of the First Amendment, the right to free speech, were outraged that Harris's and Klebold's actions were being blamed on music, movies, and games, while other people insisted that violent media have helped to create killers among the nation's youth. Defenders of the Second Amendment, the right to keep and bear arms, faced similar controversy when many survivors and victims' families called for stricter gun-control laws, blaming loose gun regulations for allowing Klebold and Harris to get their weapons easily. The National Rifle Association and other advocates of gun rights refused to blame firearms for Harris's and Klebold's violent personalities and actions.

"The people responsible for these murders are Eric Harris and Dylan Klebold," said Bill Tuthill, the acting attorney for Jefferson County during the lawsuits. "To place blame on anyone else causes only more pain and injustice."[75] Ultimately, when the lawsuits were either settled or dismissed, attention turned to the killers themselves. Eric Harris and Dylan Klebold became subjects of study for school psychologists and criminal profilers. There had been signs of trouble with Harris and Klebold long before the day of their attack—suspensions from school, violent writing assignments, offhand remarks they made to friends, and their arrest for breaking into a van. Harris and Klebold's rampage was the worst school shooting of its time, but it was not the first such incident the country had seen. Law enforcement experts began to take a closer look at the kinds of kids who were doing the shooting. If Harris and Klebold had things in common with other shooters, then schools and law enforcement might be able to identify troubled teens before things got to the point of murder and suicide.

Profiling a School Shooter

In the years since the shootings at Columbine, social scientists have tried to identify what drives some adolescents and teenagers to open fire on their peers. Statistically, a school shooter is most

Dylan Klebold fit the profile of a school shooter: a white, male teenager who was a social outcast.

77

9

Average number of school shooting incidents in American K-12 schools each year

often a white, male adolescent or teenager from a middle-class family. Both Harris and Klebold fit these characteristics. Like other school shooters who have committed similar crimes in the past several decades, Klebold and Harris were also outcasts in their school's social environment. "Students who [turn] violent are often disenfranchised from the student body," say criminal justice professors Ronald M. Holmes and Stephen T. Holmes, authors of *Murder in America*. "Other students at the school typically tell reporters and police that the shooters were 'weird' and outcasts of the student body."[76] According to sociologist and rampage shooting expert Ralph W. Larkin, who interviewed many Columbine students after the shootings, Harris and Klebold indeed gravitated toward the outcast students. One student told Larkin, "Columbine is a good, clean place except for those rejects. Most kids didn't want them here … the whole school's disgusted with them."[77]

Holmes and Holmes also say that a school shooter "will eventually abandon his former friends."[78] This, too, appears to have been true for Harris and Klebold. Former Columbine student Brooks Brown describes how his friendship with both boys grew weaker during their high school years as the two pulled away from others. "Eric and Dylan had clearly bonded much more strongly with each other than the rest of us,"[79] he says. The statistical profile of a school shooter does not mean that all white, middle-class male students with few friends will turn into school shooters just because they fit the profile. Connie Callahan, a professor of counseling and educational psychology, says, "There is no single profile of a student who may pose a real threat and no assured way to predict if a student will become violent."[80] Nevertheless, law enforcement officials learned from the shootings at Columbine that behaviors that fit the characteristics of school shooters should no longer be ignored.

The people who knew Harris and Klebold and were aware of their strange behavior seemed to believe it was a teenage phase that would soon pass. There were signs that Harris and Klebold had violent thoughts and feelings, but no one took these seriously, or at least, not seriously enough. Law enforcement agencies now teach schools how to recognize and take action about potentially violent kids.

Safe School Initiative

Two months after the shootings at Columbine High School, the U.S. Secret Service teamed up with the U.S. Department of Education on the Safe School Initiative, a program to give schools information and training on how to identify and stop potential school shooters before they become violent. The Secret Service, best known for protecting the president of the United States and other high-ranking government officials, worked with schools to help them determine what warning signs they should look for. "This process relies primarily on an assessment of behaviors, rather than on stated threats or traits, as the basis for determining whether there is cause for concern,"[81] according to *Threat Assessment in Schools: A Guide to Managing Threatening Situations and to Creating Safe School Climates*, written by the Secret Service and the Department

School officers participating in "Active Shooter" training. Many schools now hold drills where students, teachers, and officers learn how to respond during a school shooting.

of Education. The guide also says, "Rather than trying to determine the 'type' of student who may engage in targeted school violence, an inquiry should focus instead on a student's behaviors and communications to determine if that student appears to be planning or preparing for an attack."[82]

In nearly all of the cases of school shootings studied in the *Threat Assessment in Schools*, including the one at Columbine, the shooters "engaged in behaviors that caused concern to at least one person, usually an adult—and most concerned at least three people."[83] If Dylan Klebold's creative writing teacher had taken action regarding his violent writing assignment then, perhaps the shootings at Columbine could have been prevented. Helping schools recognize warning signs and teaching them how to intervene before something happens is the goal of the Safe School Initiative.

School Shooting Drills

Since the shootings at Columbine, many schools now hold school-shooting drills, similar to fire drills, in which students and teachers practice what to do in the event of a school attack. Stein says, "the safest place is in the classroom." He also says, "most schools are constructed with cinder blocks, which form a fairly secure safety barrier from bullets or from an explosion." Classroom doors can also be locked to keep out attackers. Stein adds that "the two most vulnerable locations in schools are the cafeteria and the library,"[84] open spaces that are often crowded, usually have only one main exit, and provide little or no cover from gunfire.

Just as schools should practice safety drills in the event of a shooting, Stein says local law enforcement officers should also prepare themselves for episodes of violence in their community's schools. "Both police and school personnel need to practice in the schools when students are not present,"[85] he says. Such practice is important as it allows officers to become familiar with the layout of the schools in their community, something that the SWAT teams responding to Columbine did not know. Today's officers are also being trained in how to disengage fire alarms and sprinklers in schools, two things that hindered the SWAT teams' efforts as they entered Columbine.

Shooting Déjà Vu

Regina Rohde was a freshman at Columbine High School when Eric Harris and Dylan Klebold carried out their deadly rampage. Rohde recalls being in the school cafeteria that day when the shootings started. She escaped the school without injury. Eight years later, Rohde was a graduate student at Virginia Tech in Blacksburg, Virginia, when a single shooter killed thirty-three people on the campus. Rohde was not on campus when the killings happened. Just the same, she told *U.S. News & World Report*, the occasions were strikingly similar. "I know what that pure terror is when you're fleeing for your life," she says, "and I can understand the grief and the anger."

At the time, in 1999, the massacre at Columbine was the deadliest school shooting that had ever taken place in America. As of 2009, the shooting at Virginia Tech in 2007 remains the deadliest mass shooting in U.S. history. The chances that Regina Rohde would attend both of the schools where the nation's deadliest rampage shootings have taken place were so small as to be nonexistent—almost.

Quoted in Chris Wilson, "Now at Va. Tech, Columbine Grads Relive Tragedy," *U.S. News & World Report*, April 17, 2007, www.usnews.com/usnews/news/articles/070417/17columbine.htm.

"A Wake-Up Call"

The need for precautions that safeguard schools from student shooters is an unfortunate reality today. There have been dozens of school shooting incidents in the United States since the massacre at Columbine. "The Columbine High School massacre was, at the time, the deadliest school shooting in the country's history," says Alex Kingsbury, a journalist for *U.S. News & World Report*, "but the number, frequency, and death toll for shootings at schools has increased dramatically since the attack at Colorado's Columbine High School."[86] The massacre at Columbine was America's deadliest school shooting for

A memorial for 23-year-old Cho Seung-Hui, who killed 32 people and himself at Virginia Tech in 2007.

only eight years. It's standing was shattered in April 2007 by a single shooter at Virginia Polytechnic Institute (Virginia Tech) in Blacksburg, Virginia, who opened fire on students in dormitories and a classroom, killing thirty-three before shooting himself. The killer, twenty-three-year-old Cho Seung-Hui, left behind a manifesto in which he wrote the phrase, "Generation after generation, we martyrs like Eric and Dylan."[87]

The events at Columbine horrified and unified the nation, and schools, law enforcement, parents, and students across the country learned to be more vigilant and to take action if they think a school or its students are in danger. "The good news in this is Columbine was a wake-up call for all of America," says Pete Pochowski, executive director of the National Association of School Safety and Law Enforcement Officers. "We are much more aware of how vulnerable our schools and our children are."[88] The Columbine shootings and the extensive investigation that followed are among the most intensely studied events in America's history.

Notes

Chapter 1: The Emergency Response

1. Barry A. J. Fisher, *Techniques of Crime Scene Investigation*, Boca Raton, FL: CRC Press, 2004, p. 143.

2. David B. Stein, "School Shootings and School Terrorist Attacks: Identification, Intervention, and Tactical Response," in *Public Policing in the 21st Century*, eds. James F. Hodgson and Catherine Orban, Monsey, NY: Criminal Justice Press, 2005, pp. 155–184, 172.

3. Jefferson County Sheriff's Office, "Sheriff's Office Final Report on the Columbine High School Shootings," http://extras.denverpost.com/news/colreport/Columbinerep/Pages/INTRO_TEXT2.htm.

4. Nancy Gibbs, Timothy Roche, Andrew Goldstein, Maureen Harrington, and Richard Woodbury, "The Columbine Tapes," *TIME*, December 20, 1999, www.time.com/time/magazine/article/0,9171,992873,00.html.

5. Dennis R. Krebs, *When Violence Erupts: A Survival Guide for Emergency Responders*, Sudbury, MA: Jones and Bartlett, 2003, p. 124.

6. Stein, "School Shootings and School Terrorist Attacks," p. 173.

7. Krebs, *When Violence Erupts*, p. 125.

8. Stein, "School Shootings and School Terrorist Attacks," p. 173.

9. Gibbs et al., "Columbine Tapes."

Chapter 2: Processing the Scene

10. TheDenverChannel.com, "Judge Throws Out Columbine Lawsuits," TheDenverChannel.com, November 21, 2001, www.thedenverchannel.com/news/1093436/detail.html.

11. Krebs, *When Violence Erupts*, p. 122.

12. Jefferson County Sheriff's Office, "Sheriff's Office Final Report on the Columbine High School Shootings."

13. David Dolinak, Evan W. Matshes, and Emma O. Lew, *Forensic Pathology: Principles and Practice*, Burlington, MA: Academic Press, 2003, p. 290.

14. Fisher, *Techniques of Crime Scene Investigation*, p. 50.

15. Ross M. Gardner, *Practical Crime Scene Processing and Investigation*, Boca Raton, FL: CRC Press, 2005, p. 3.

16. Gardner, *Practical Crime Scene Processing*, p. 125.

17. Gardner, *Practical Crime Scene Processing*, p. 118.

18. Richard H. Walton, *Cold Case Homicides: Practical Investigative Techniques*, Boca Raton, FL: CRC Press, 2006, pp. 443–44.

19. Stuart James, Paul Kish, and E. Paulette Sutton, *Principles of Bloodstain Pattern Analysis: Theory and Practice*, Boca Raton, FL: CRC Press, 2005, pp. 138–39.

20. Louis L. Akin, "Blood Spatter Interpretation at Crime and Accident Scenes: A Basic Approach," *FBI Law Enforcement Bulletin*, February 2005, www.fbi.gov/publications/leb/2005/feb2005/feb2005.htm#page21.

21. Ian Prior, "The Ballistics Expert at the Scene," in *The Practice of Crime Scene Investigation*, ed. John Horswell, Boca Raton, FL: 2004, pp. 181–94, 188.

22. Prior, "Ballistics Expert at the Scene," p. 188.

23. Prior, "Ballistics Expert at the Scene," p. 188.

24. Dan Luzadder and Kevin Vaughan, "Inside the Columbine Investigation," *Denver Rocky Mountain News*, December 12, 1999, http://denver.rockymountainnews.com/shooting/1212col1.shtml.

25. Jefferson County Sheriff's Office, "Sheriff's Office Final Report on the Columbine High School Shootings."

26. Jefferson County Sheriff's Office, "Sheriff's Office Final Report on the Columbine High School Shootings."

27. Barry Fisher, David Fisher, and David Kolowski, *Forensics Demystified: A Self-Teaching Guide*, New York: McGraw-Hill, 2007, p. 82.

28. Jefferson County Sheriff's Office, "Sheriff's Office Final Report on the Columbine High School Shootings."

29. Jefferson County Sheriff's Office, "Sheriff's Office Final Report on the Columbine High School Shootings."

Chapter 3: The Killers

30. Jefferson County Sheriff's Office, "Sheriff's Office Final Report on the Columbine High School Shootings."

31. Jefferson County Sheriff's Office, "Sheriff's Office Final Report on the Columbine High School Shootings."

32. Brooks Brown and Rob Merritt, *No Easy Answers: The Truth Behind Death at Columbine*, New York: Lantern, 2002, pp. 70–71.

33. Quoted in Gibbs et al., "Columbine Tapes."

34. Quoted in Jeff Kass, *Columbine: A True Crime Story*, Denver, CO: Ghost Road Press, 2009, p. 139.

35. Quoted in Kass, *Columbine*, p. 159.

36. Glenn W. Muschert and Ralph W. Larkin, "The Columbine High School Shootings," in *Crimes and Trials of the Century*, eds. Steven M. Chermak and Frankie Y. Bailey, Westport, CT: Greenwood, 2007, pp. 253–66, 256.

37. Jefferson County Sheriff's Office, "Sheriff's Office Final Report on the Columbine High School Shootings."

38. Kass, *Columbine*, p. 106.

39. Brown and Merritt, *No Easy Answers*, p. 72.

40. Brown and Merritt, *No Easy Answers*, p. 72.

41. Brown and Merritt, *No Easy Answers*, p. 73.

42. Quoted in Gibbs et al., "Columbine Tapes."

43. Quoted in Kass, *Columbine*, p. 154.

44. Ralph W. Larkin, *Comprehending Columbine*, Philadelphia, PA: Temple University Press, 2007, p. 129.

45. Quoted in Gibbs et al., "Columbine Tapes."

46. Jefferson County Sheriff's Office, "Sheriff's Office Final Report on the Columbine High School Shootings."

47. Jefferson County Sheriff's Office, "Sheriff's Office Final Report on the Columbine High School Shootings."

48. Susan Greene and Bill Briggs, "Attention Focuses on 'Trench Coat Mafia,'" *Denver Post*, April 21, 1999, http://extras.denverpost.com/news/shot0420e.htm.

49. Jefferson County Sheriff's Office, "Sheriff's Office Final Report on the Columbine High School Shootings."

50. Jefferson County Sheriff's Office, "Sheriff's Office Final Report on the Columbine High School Shootings."

Chapter 4: The Weapons

51. Quoted in Dave Cullen, *Columbine*, New York: Twelve, 2009, p. 234.

52. Peter G. Chronis and David Olinger, "Killers' Pistol Akin to Banned Model," *Denver Post*, April 23, 1999, http://extras.denverpost.com/news/shot0423b.htm.

53. Chronis and Olinger, "Killers' Pistol Akin to Banned Model."

54. Jefferson County Sheriff's Office, "Sheriff's Office Final Report on the Columbine High School Shootings."

55. Quoted in Kass, *Columbine*, p. 127.

56. Quoted in Kass, *Columbine*, p. 135.

57. Quoted in Kass, *Columbine*, p. 134.

58. Ann Carnahan and John C. Ensslin, "Jeffco Man Arrested in Gun Sale," *Denver Rocky Mountain News*, May 4, 1999, http://denver.rockymountainnews.com/shooting/0504gung0.shtml.

59. Quoted in Cullen, *Columbine*, p. 276.

60. Jefferson County Sheriff's Office, "Sheriff's Office Final Report on the Columbine High School Shootings."

61. Jefferson County Sheriff's Office, "Sheriff's Office Final Report on the Columbine High School Shootings."

62. John R. Cashman, *Emergency Response Handbook for Chemical and Biological Agents and Weapons*, Boca Raton, FL: CRC Press, 2008, p. 57.

63. Cullen, *Columbine*, p. 351.

64. Quoted in Kevin Simpson, "Columbine Gives Explosive Lesson," *Denver Post*, July 26, 1999, http://extras.denverpost.com/news/shot0726b.htm.

65. Quoted in Gibbs et al., "Columbine Tapes."

66. Gibbs et al., "Columbine Tapes."

Chapter 5: Lessons Learned

67. Quoted in Jefferson County Sheriff's Office, "Sheriff's Office Final Report on the Columbine High School Shootings."

68. Quoted in Kass, *Columbine*, p. 123.

69. Cullen, *Columbine*, p. 57.

70. Stein, "School Shootings and School Terrorist Attacks," p. 171.

71. Stein, "School Shootings and School Terrorist Attacks," p. 155.

72. Darcia Harris Bowman, "Police Adopt 'Rapid Response' to Shootings," *Education Week*, April 4, 2001. www.edweek.org/ew/articles/2001/04/04/29secure.h20.html.

73. Bowman, "Police Adopt 'Rapid Response.'"

74. Quoted in Bowman, "Police Adopt 'Rapid Response.'"

75. Quoted in Denver Channel News, "Judge Throws Out Columbine Lawsuits," November 27, 2001, www.thedenverchannel.com/news/1093436/detail.html.

76. Ronald M. Holmes and Stephen T. Holmes, *Murder in America*, 2nd ed., Thousand Oaks, CA: Sage, 2001, p. 91.

77. Quoted in Larkin, *Comprehending Columbine*, p. 103.

78. Holmes and Holmes, *Murder in America*, p. 94.

79. Brown and Merritt, *No Easy Answers*, p. 70.

80. Connie Callahan, "Threat Assessment in School Violence," in *School Violence and Primary Prevention*, ed. Thomas W. Miller, New York: Springer, 2008, pp. 59–78, 60.

81. U.S. Secret Service and U.S. Department of Education, *Threat Assessment in Schools: A Guide to Managing Threatening Situations and to Creating Safe School Climates*, Washington, DC: Authors, 2002, p. 5.

82. Secret Service and Department of Education, *Threat Assessment in Schools*, p. 21.

83. Secret Service and Department of Education, *Threat Assessment in Schools*, p. 21.

84. Stein, "School Shootings and School Terrorist Attacks," p. 172.

85. Stein, "School Shootings and School Terrorist Attacks," p. 180.

86. Alex Kingsbury, "After Columbine, School Shootings Proliferate," *U.S. News & World Report*, April 17, 2007, www.usnews.com/usnews/news/articles/070417/17shootings.htm.

87. Quoted in Howard Berkes, Barbara Bradley Hagerty, and Jennifer Ludden, "NBC Defends Release of Va. Tech Gunman Video," National Public Radio, April 18, 2007, www.npr.org/templates/story/story.php?storyId=9604204.

88. Quoted in Amy Hetzner, "A Decade After Columbine, School Security Remains High Priority," *Milwaukee Wisconsin Journal Sentinel*, April 19, 2009, www.jsonline.com/news/education/43257637.html.

Glossary

accomplice: A person who helps someone else commit a crime.

ATF: Short for the Bureau of Alcohol, Tobacco, Firearms and Explosives; the agency within the Department of Justice that regulates guns, explosives, and controlled substances and investigates crimes that involve them.

autopsy: An examination of a body to determine cause of death.

ballistics: The study of bullets once they are fired from a gun.

blood spatter analysis: The interpretation of how blood from an injured person travels through the air to make patterns on surrounding objects, indicating the direction and type of the impact that caused the injury.

bomb squad: A team of crime scene technicians experienced in safely handling explosive devices.

coroner: A public official who investigates causes of a death once natural causes are ruled out.

critical incident: An overwhelming and emotional emergency situation that demands help from many responders.

felony: A serious crime, punished by time in prison.

in situ: In the original position, not having been moved.

rapid response: An immediate response to an emergency, especially an immediate police response to engage an active shooter.

Red Cross: An international organization that provides resources and assistance for people during disasters.

Salvation Army: A charitable organization that provides help and support to people in need.

search warrant: A legal document authorizing police to search someone's personal property in search of illegal possessions or evidence of a crime.

staging area: A safe place, away from the scene of a crime or disaster, where emergency responders can set up their teams and equipment as they prepare to enter the scene.

SWAT team: Short for Special Weapons and Tactics, SWAT teams are teams of police officers who carry powerful weapons and are specially trained to deal with unusually violent or dangerous situations.

For More Information

Books

Judy L. Hasday, *Columbine High School Shooting: Student Violence*. Berkeley Heights, NJ: Enslow, 2002. This book presents the facts about the shootings at Columbine High School and includes an illustrated time line of the forty-five-minute attack on the school.

Susan C. Hunnicut, ed., *At Issue: School Shootings*. Farmington Hills, MI: Greenhaven Press, 2006. This collection of articles and reports by eyewitnesses, scientists, government officials, and others addresses the complicated issue of school violence from a variety of perspectives.

Periodicals

Jessica Calefati, "A Survivor's Story: 10 Years After Columbine, *U.S. News & World Report*, April 17, 2009, www.usnews.com/articles/education/2009/04/17/a-survivors-story-10-years-after-columbine.html.

Adam Cohen, Harriet Barovick, Desa Philadelphia, Elaine Rivera, Laura Laughlin, Jodie Morse, and David Nordan, "A Curse of Cliques," *TIME*, May 3, 1999, www.time.com/time/magazine/article/0,9171,990871,00.html.

Denver Post, "Columbine: Where They Are Now," *Denver Post*, April 19, 2009, www.denverpost.com/columbine/ci_12174129.

Bruce D. Perry, "Columbine, Killing, and You," Scholastic, http://teacher.scholastic.com/professional/bruceperry/columbine_killing.htm.

DVDs

"The Columbine Shootings." *ABC News Classics*. DVD. New York: ABC News, 2007. Featuring forty-five minutes of the original news coverage broadcast the day of the Columbine shootings, this video captures the confusion and panic surrounding the school during the rampage.

"Columbine—Understanding Why." *Investigative Reports*. DVD. New York: A&E Home Video, 2008. Led by a forensic psychiatrist, this investigation into the Columbine murder spree focuses on the killers and what motivated them to open fire on their peers.

Web Sites

Denver Post.com (http://extras.denverpost.com/news/shotmain.htm). This Web site contains a section called "Columbine

Tragedy and Recovery" that includes links to the articles printed in the *Denver Post* newspaper in the days, weeks, and months after the attack at Columbine High School, as well as the text of the Jefferson County Sheriff's Office official report on the shootings.

United States Secret Service (www .secretservice.gov/ntac_ssi.shtml). The National Threat Assessment Center on the U.S. Secret Service's Web site offers information on the Secret Service Safe School Initiative as well as tips for students and teachers to stay safe.

Index

Picture Credits

Cover photo: Mark Leffingwell/Getty Images

AP Images, 9, 23, 28, 32, 35, 44, 45, 49, 51, 60, 62, 71, 72, 75, 77, 79

Getty Images News/Getty Images, 37, 53

Jeff Haynes/AFP/Getty Images, 41

© Kim Kulish/Corbis, 73

Larry W. Smith/Getty Images, 13

Mark Leffingwell/AFP/Getty Images, 17

Mark Leffingwell/Getty Images, 11, 67

© N. Warren Winter/ZUMA/Corbis, 64

© Rick Maiman/Sygma/Corbis, 55

Scott Olson/Getty Images, 82

© Steve Starr/Corbis, 24

© Tom Cooper/Sygma/Corbis, 15, 20

About the Author

Jenny MacKay is a freelance writer and editor and the author of seven nonfiction books for teens. She is currently pursuing her master's degree in creative writing. She lives with her husband and two children in northern Nevada, where she was born and raised.